PASTEL PAINTING OF THE 30 AMAZING CARS

ILLUSTRATED BY PETER WONG

Copyright © 2024 Peter Wong
All rights reserved.
ISBN-9798335596435

No part of this book maybe reproduced, transmitted or stored in any form or by any means except for a book review, without the express written permission of the author. Contact us: hellomocalife@gmail.com

Introduction

Let's explore the current development and trends of amazing automobile design.
The illustrator, Peter Wong, carefully collected information and drew with pastel
expression techniques to represent the design work.

We will unfold the development status of special products and
learn to use pastel techniques to achieve the ability to express creativity quickly.

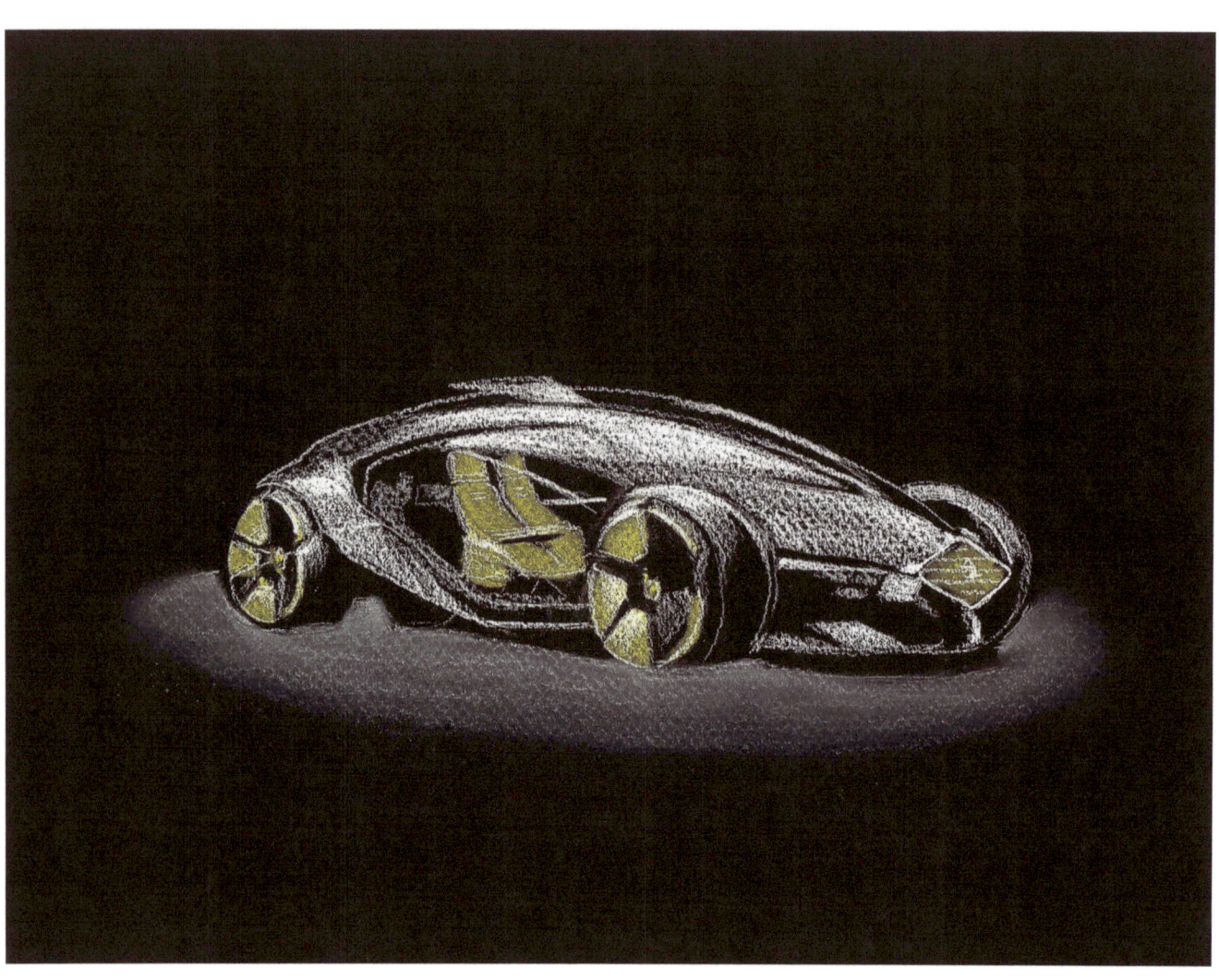

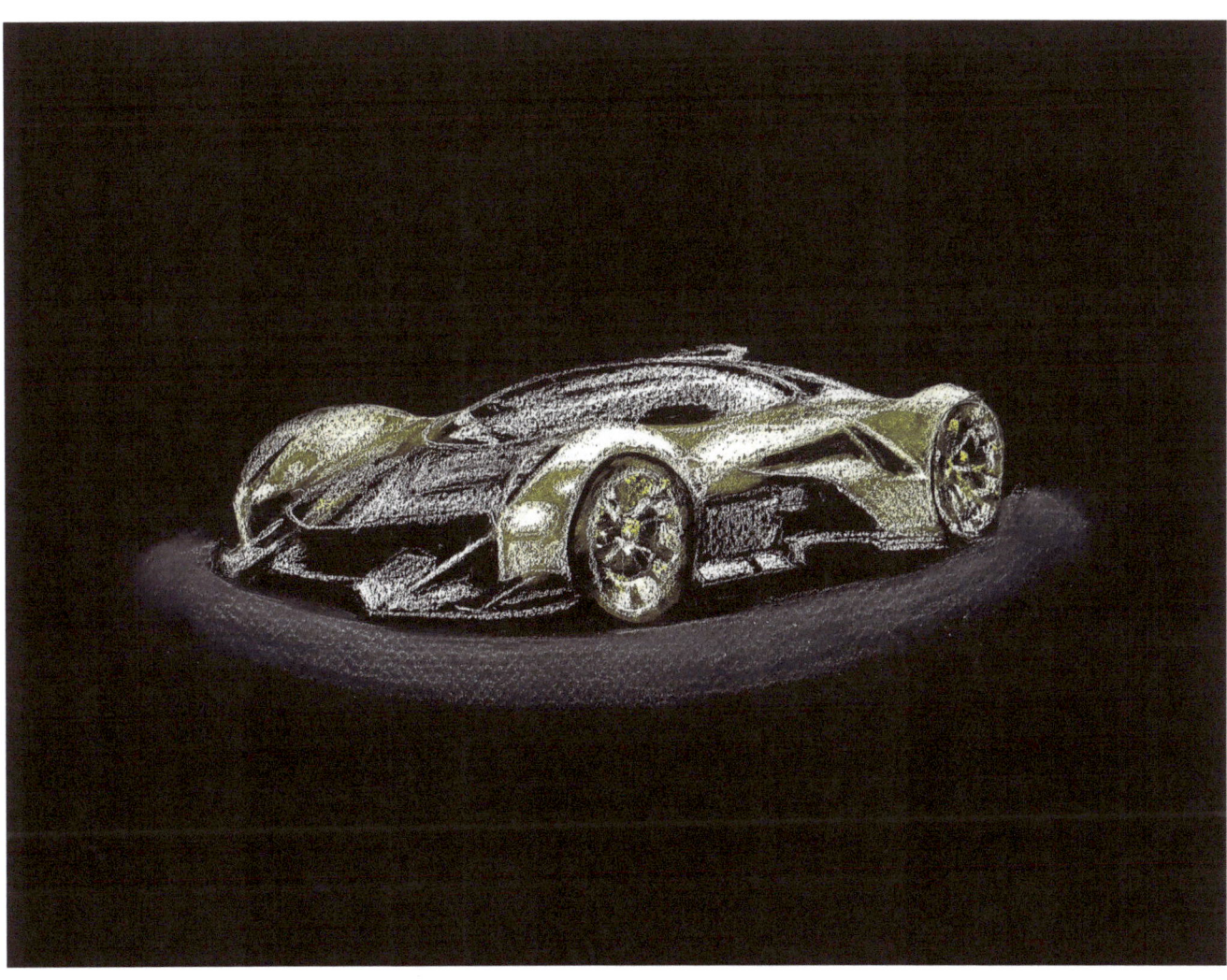

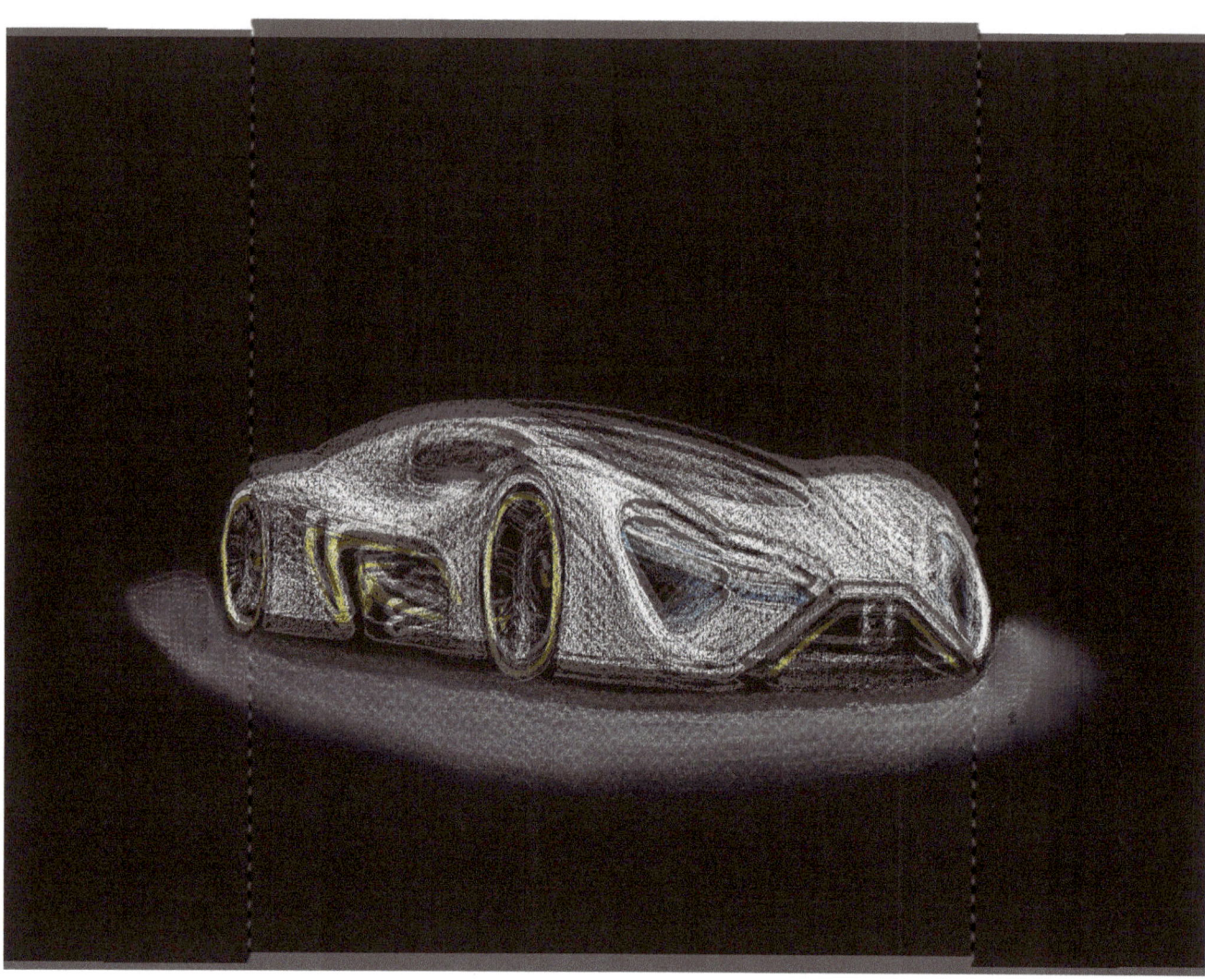

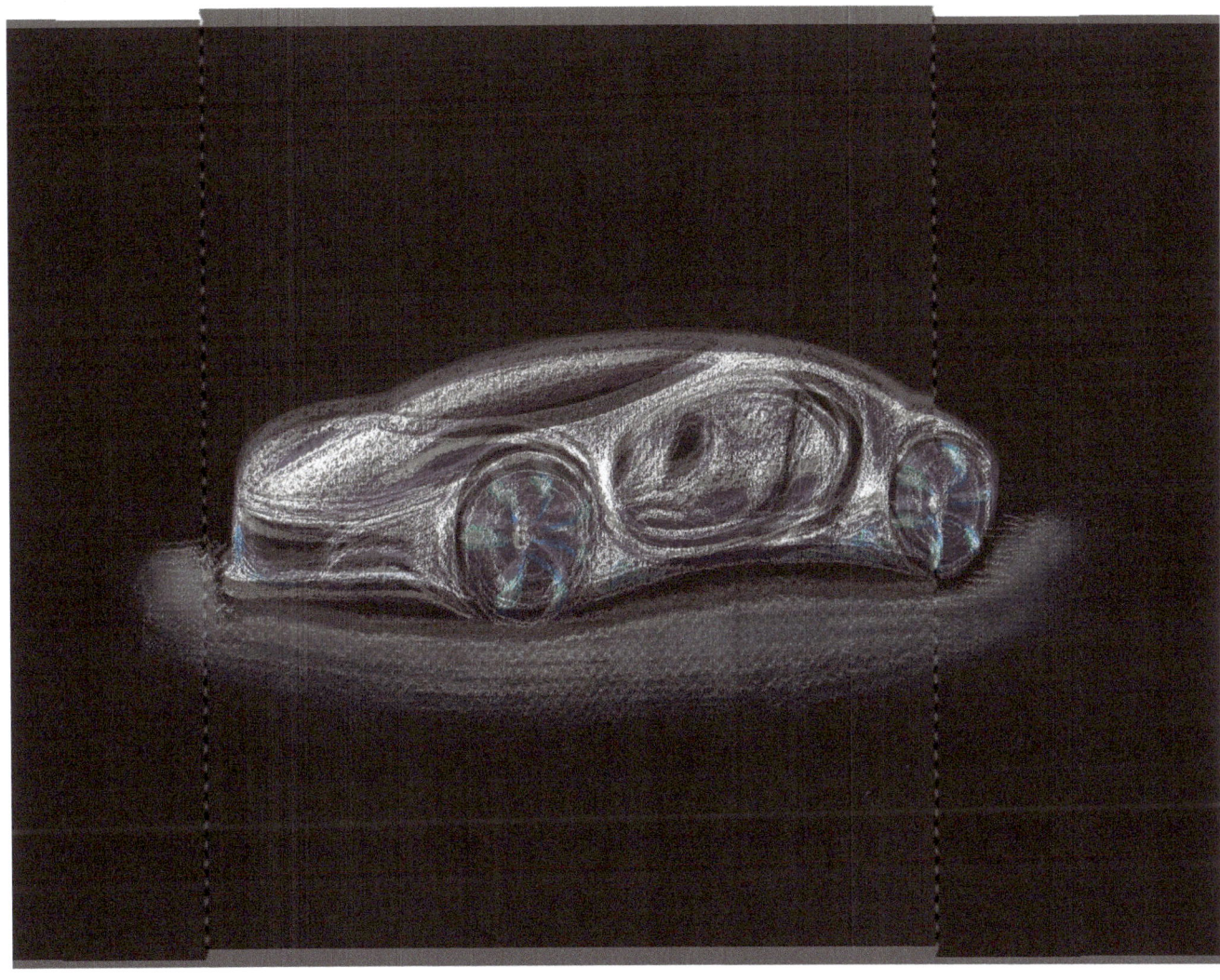

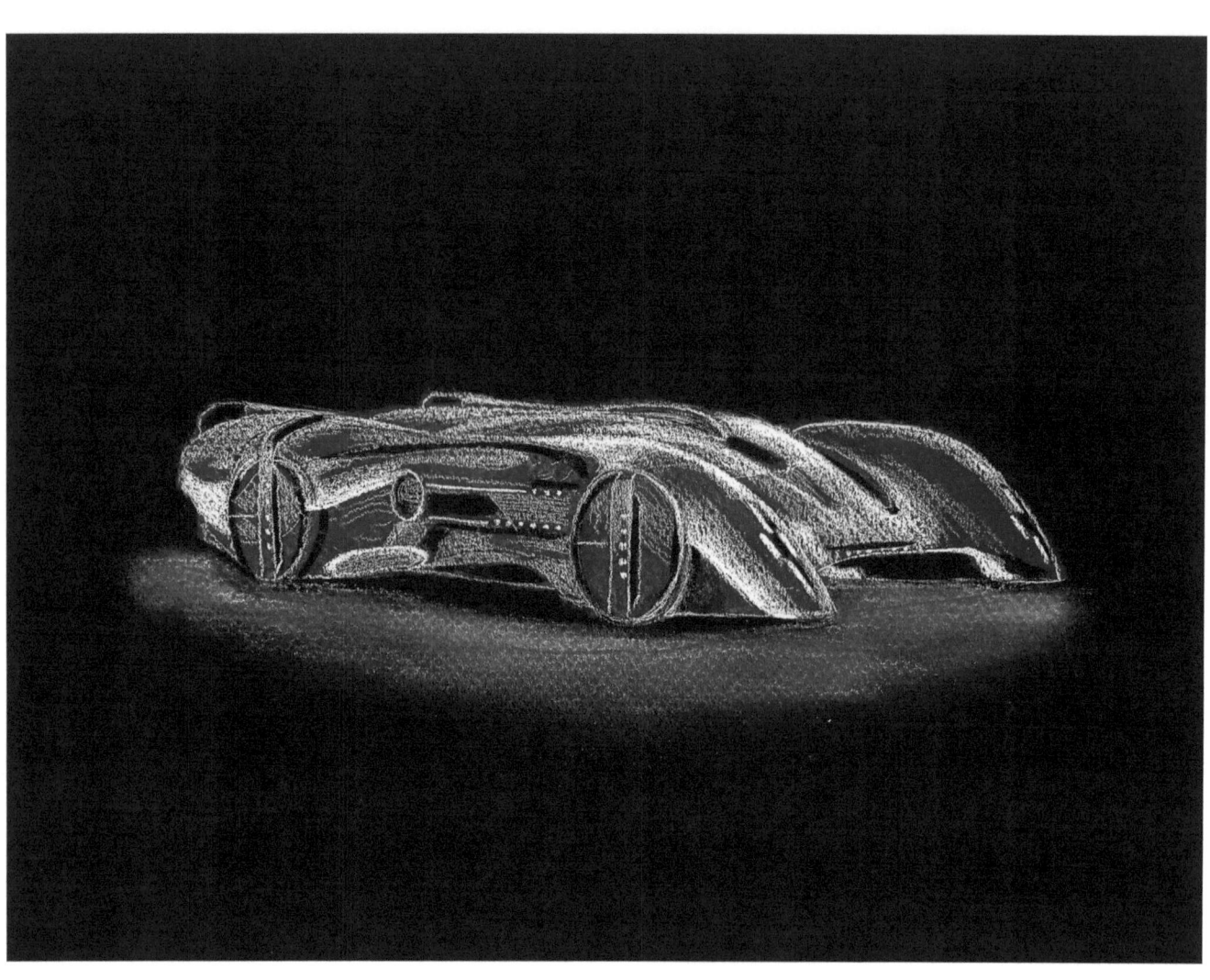

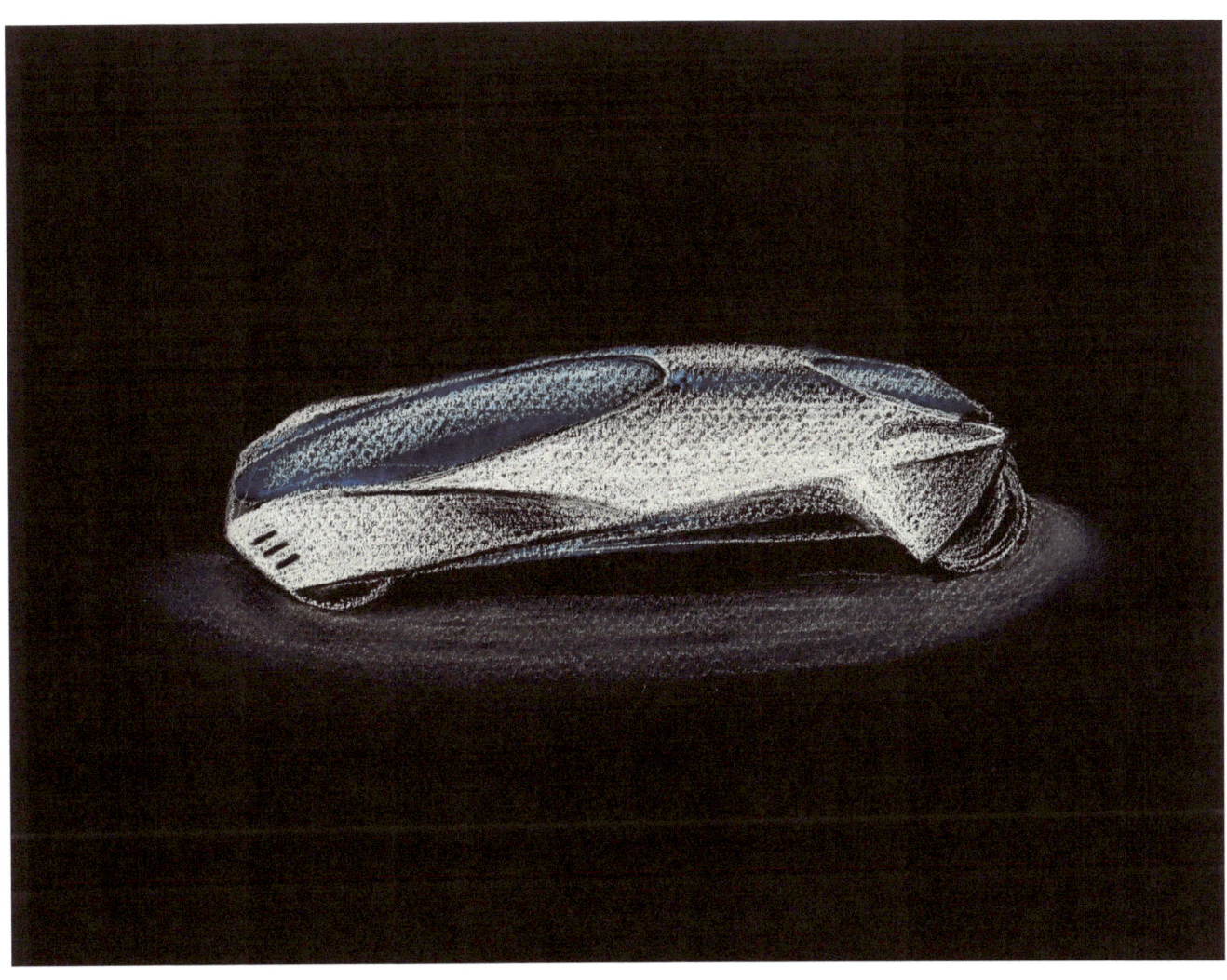

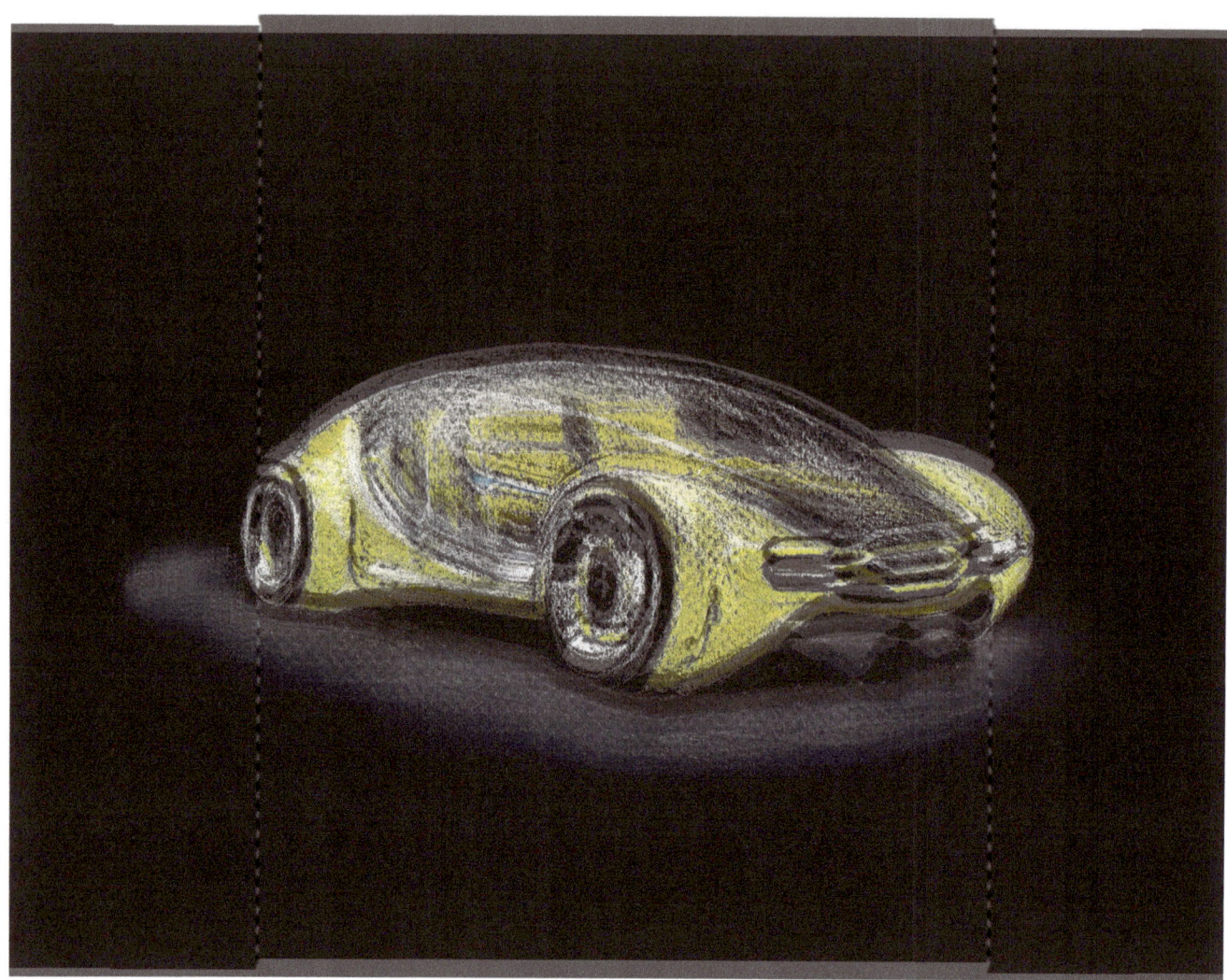

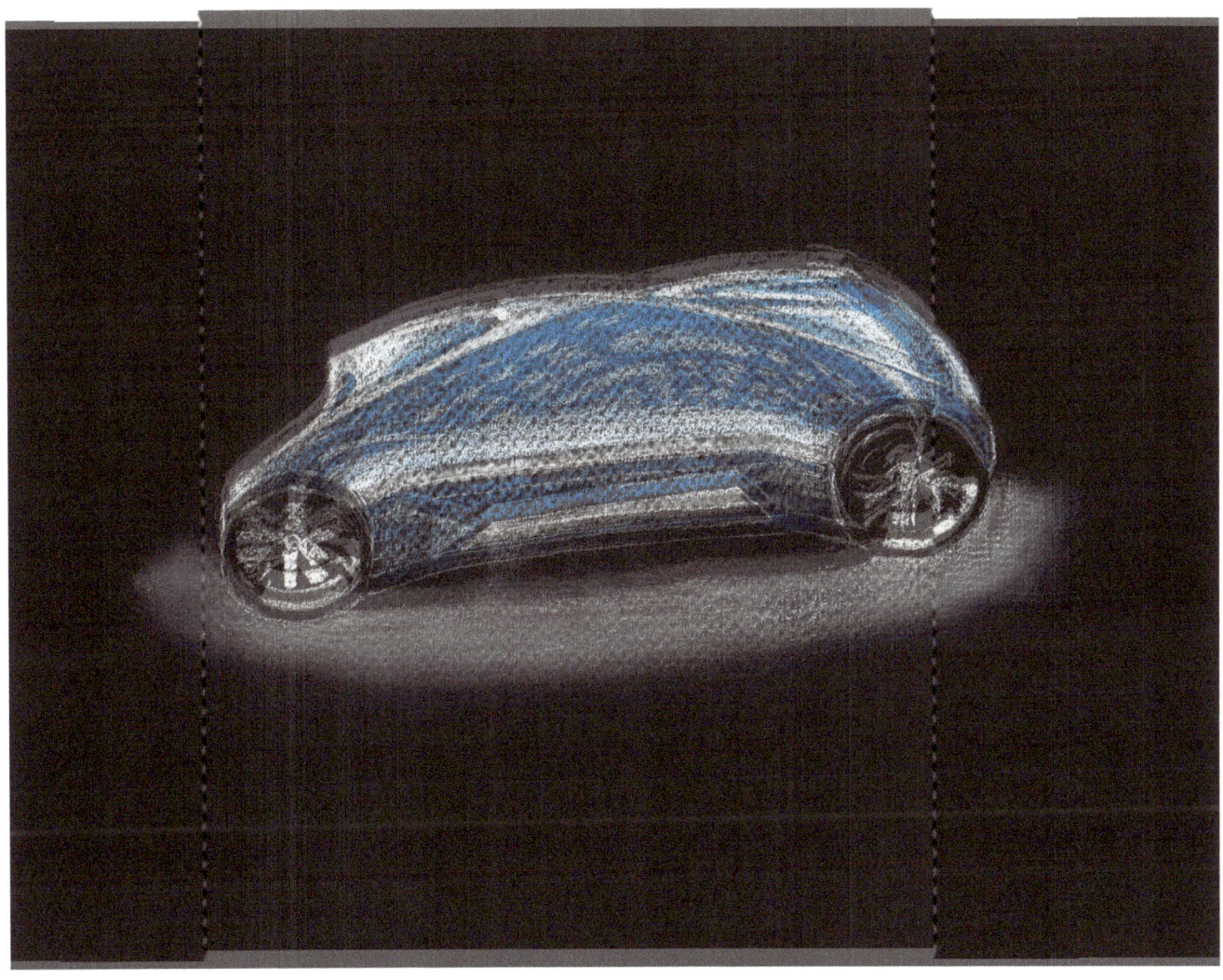

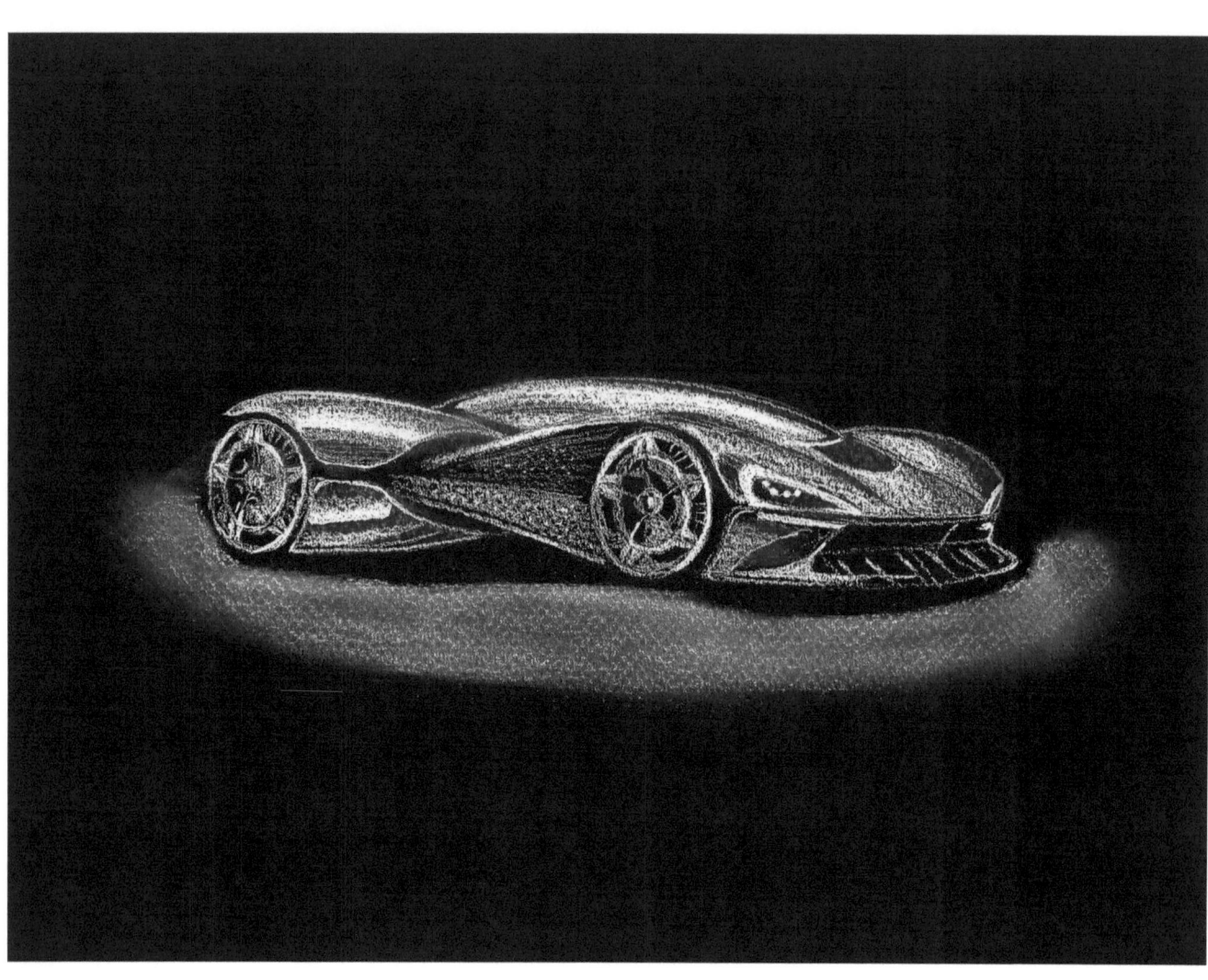

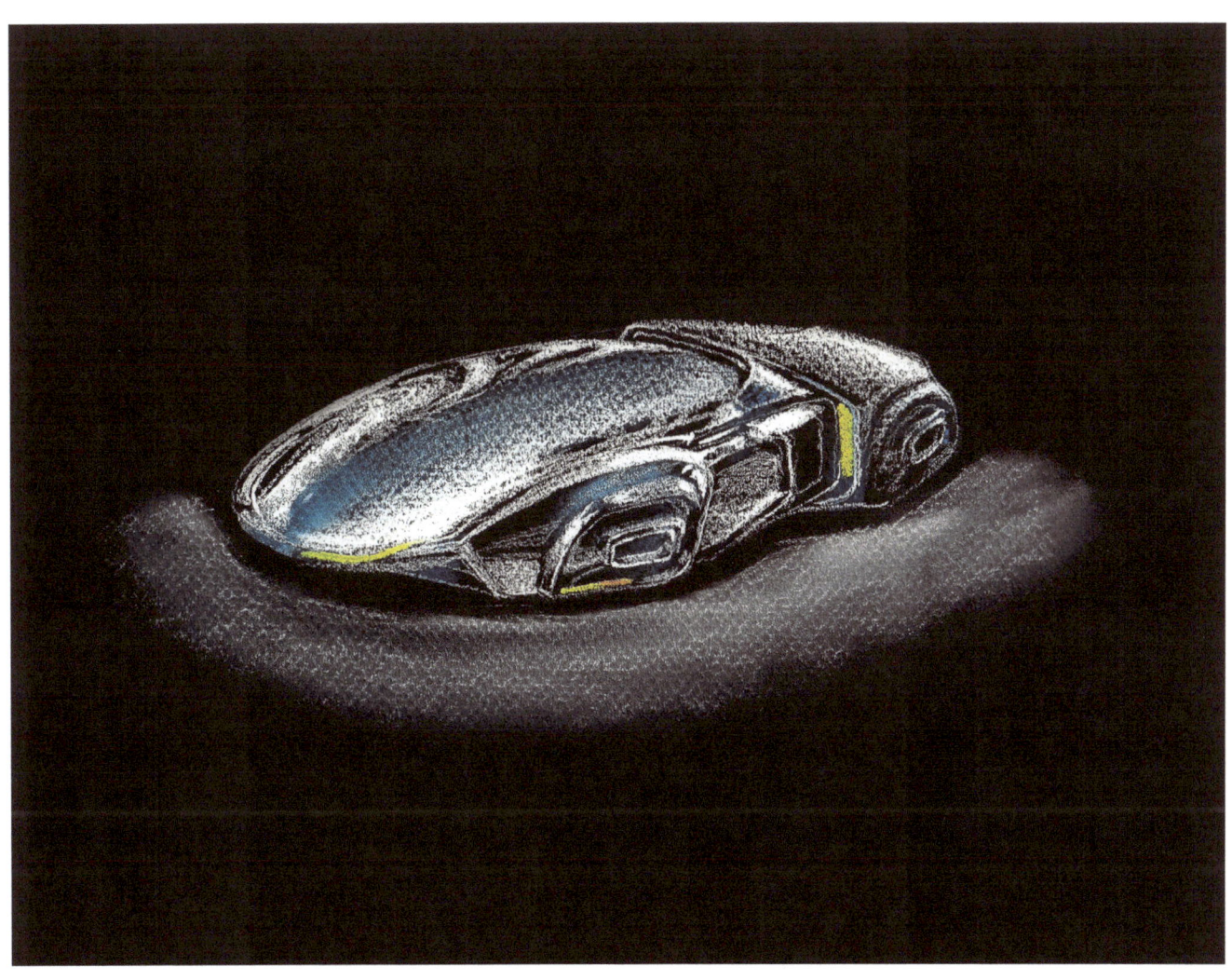

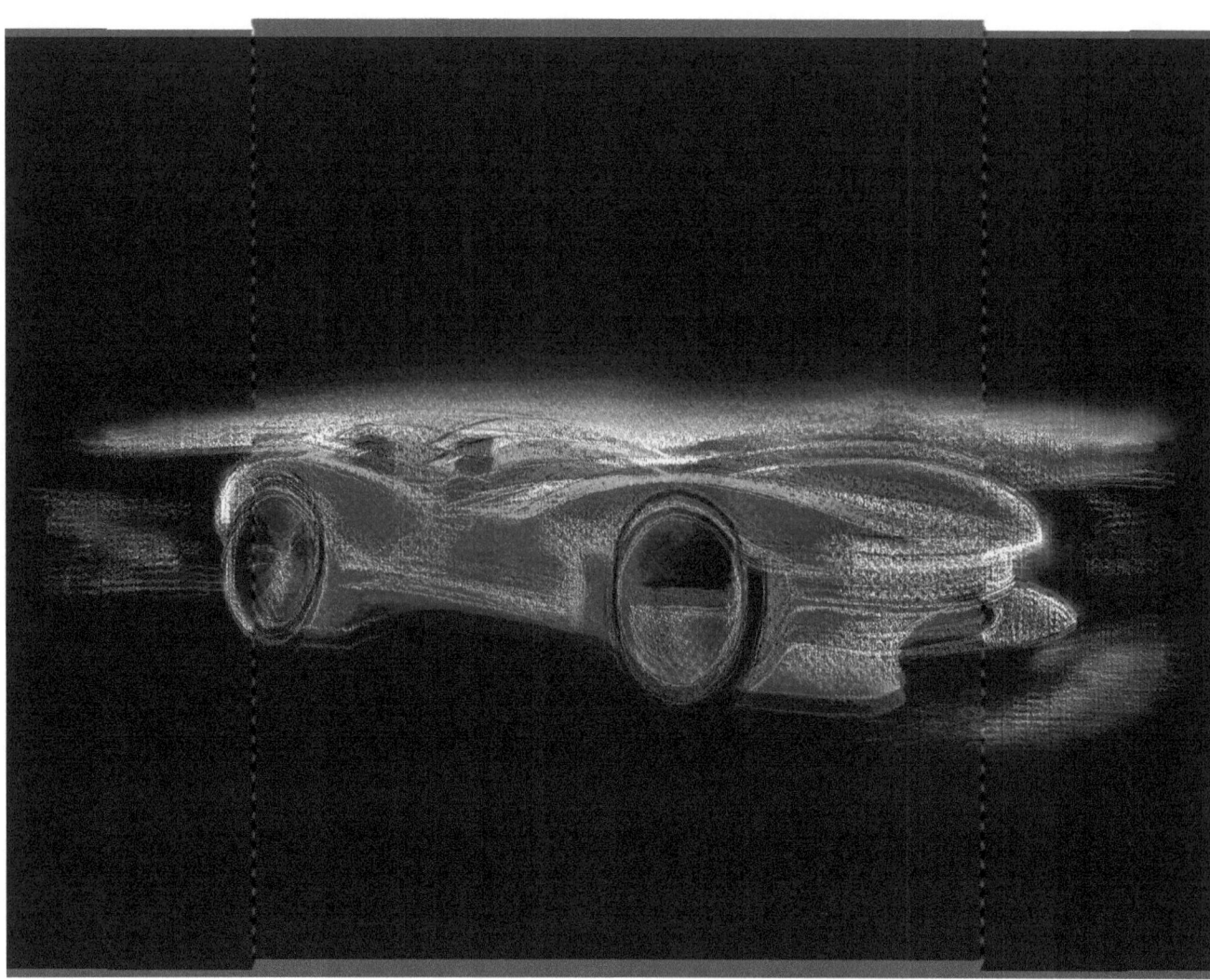

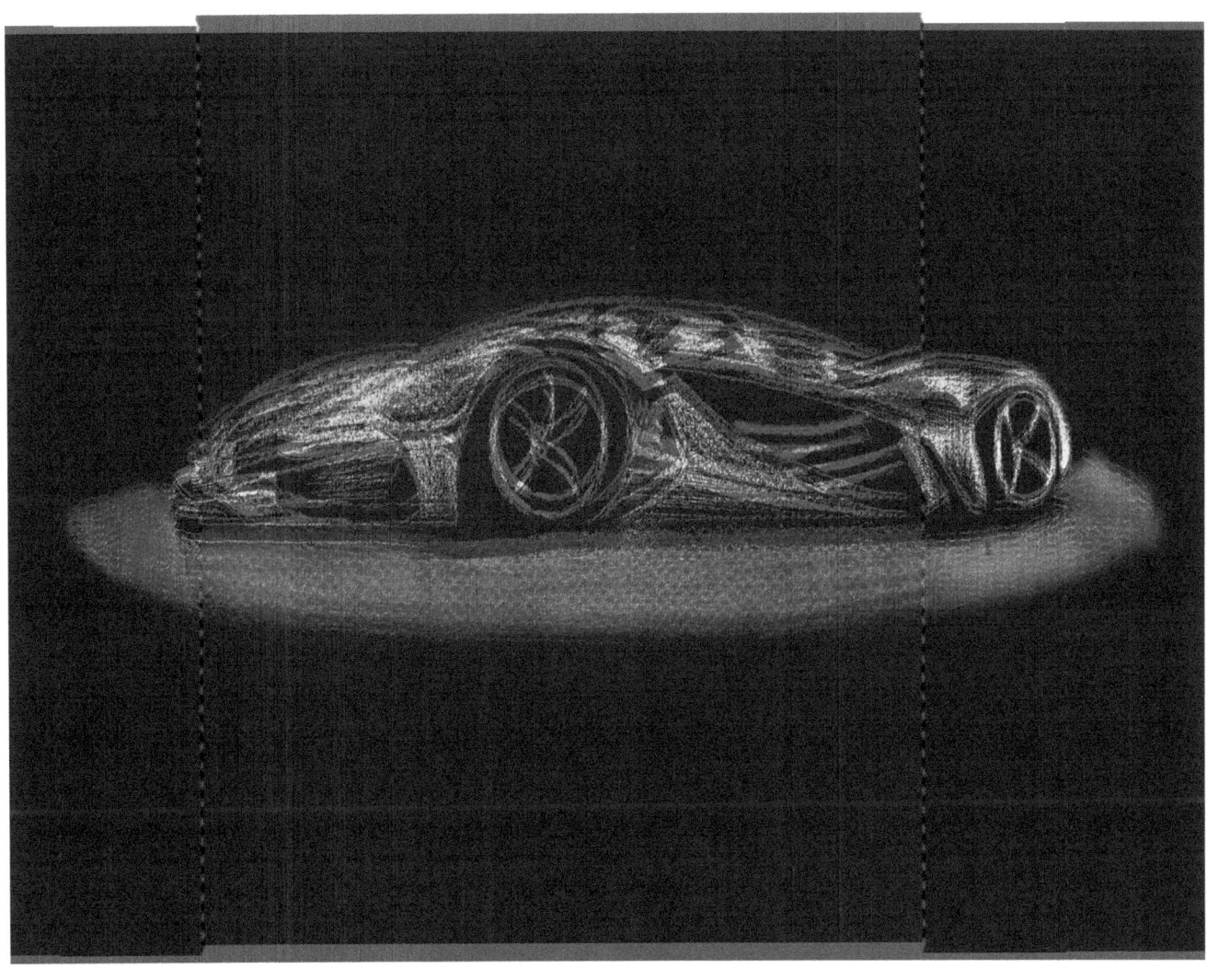

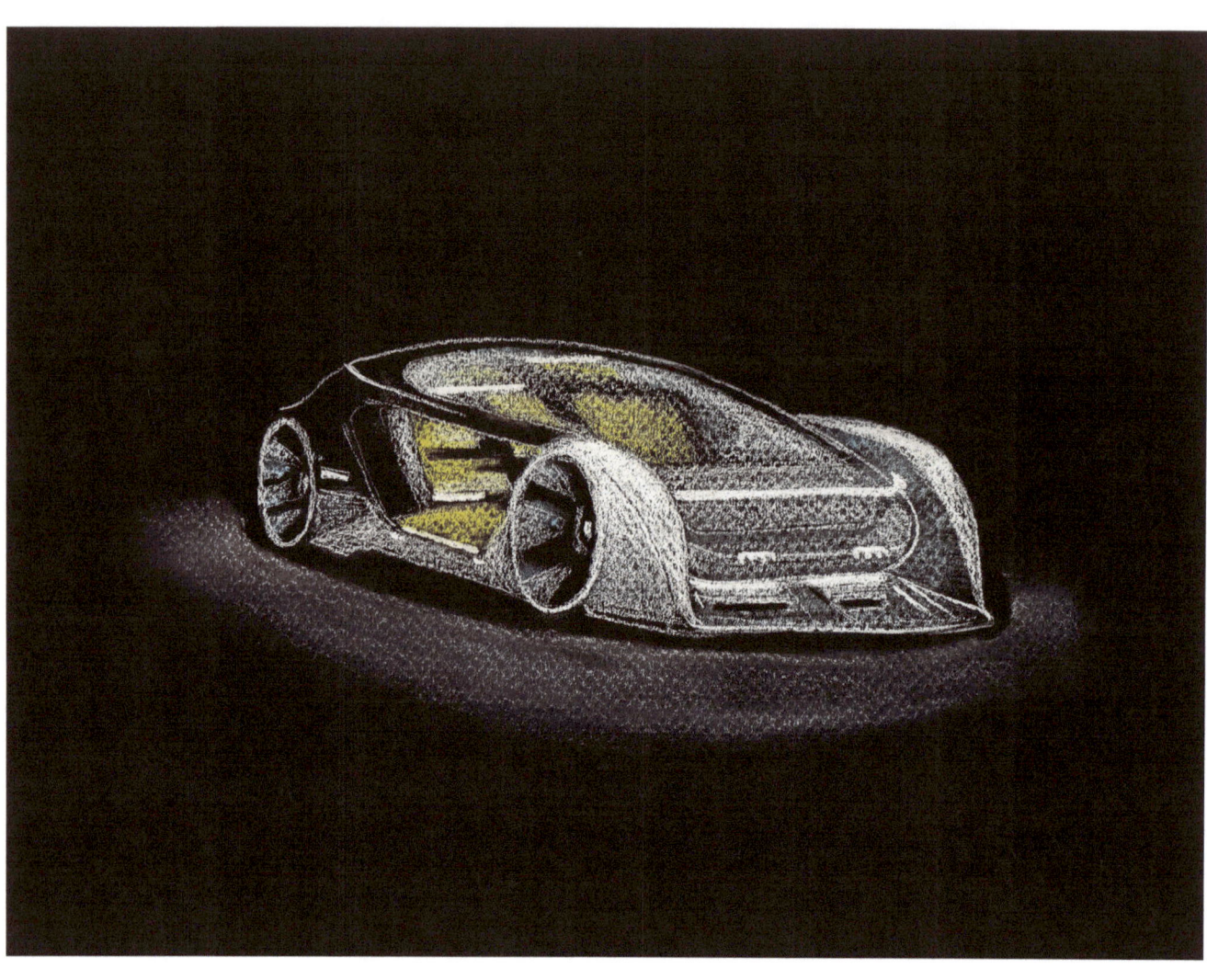

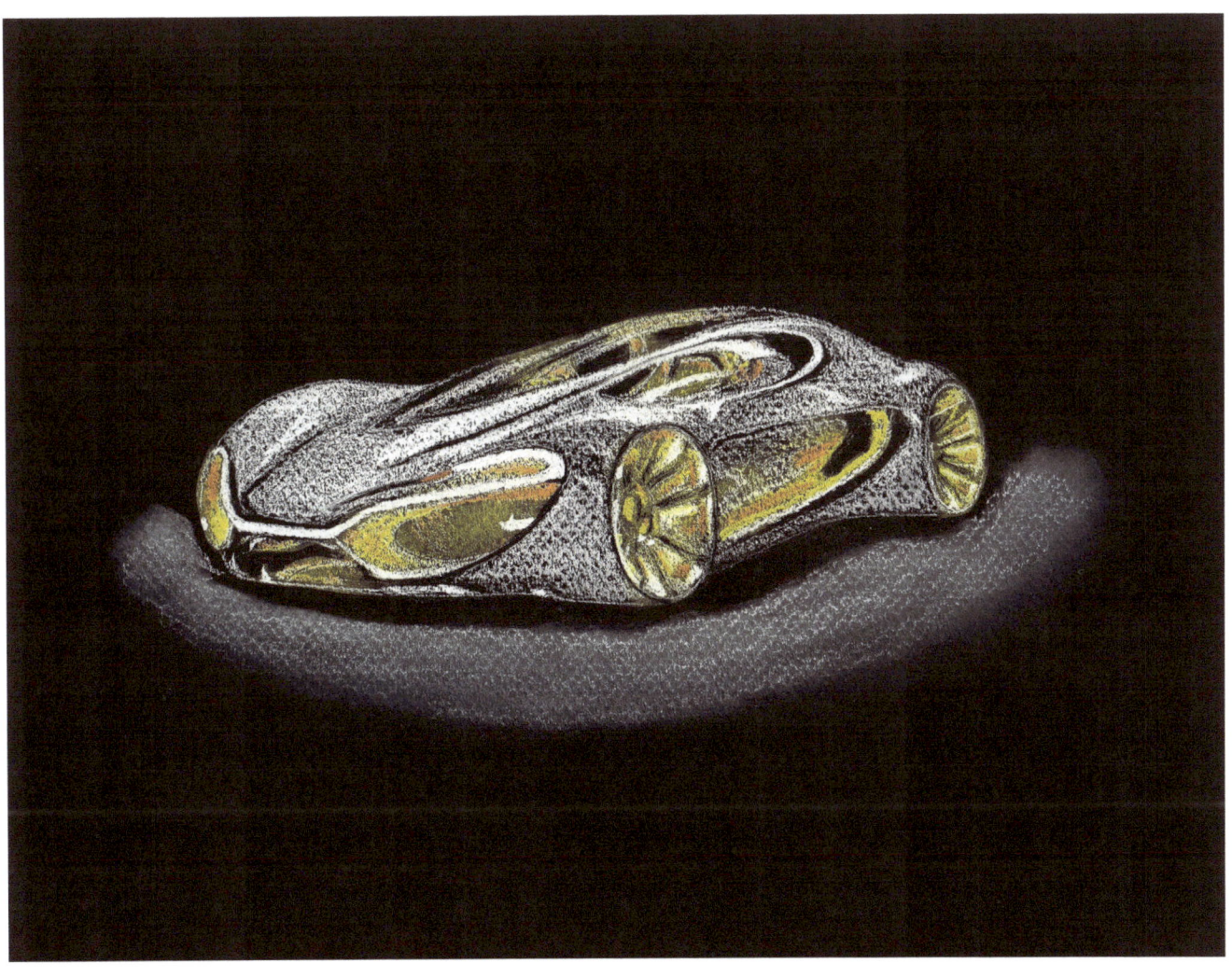

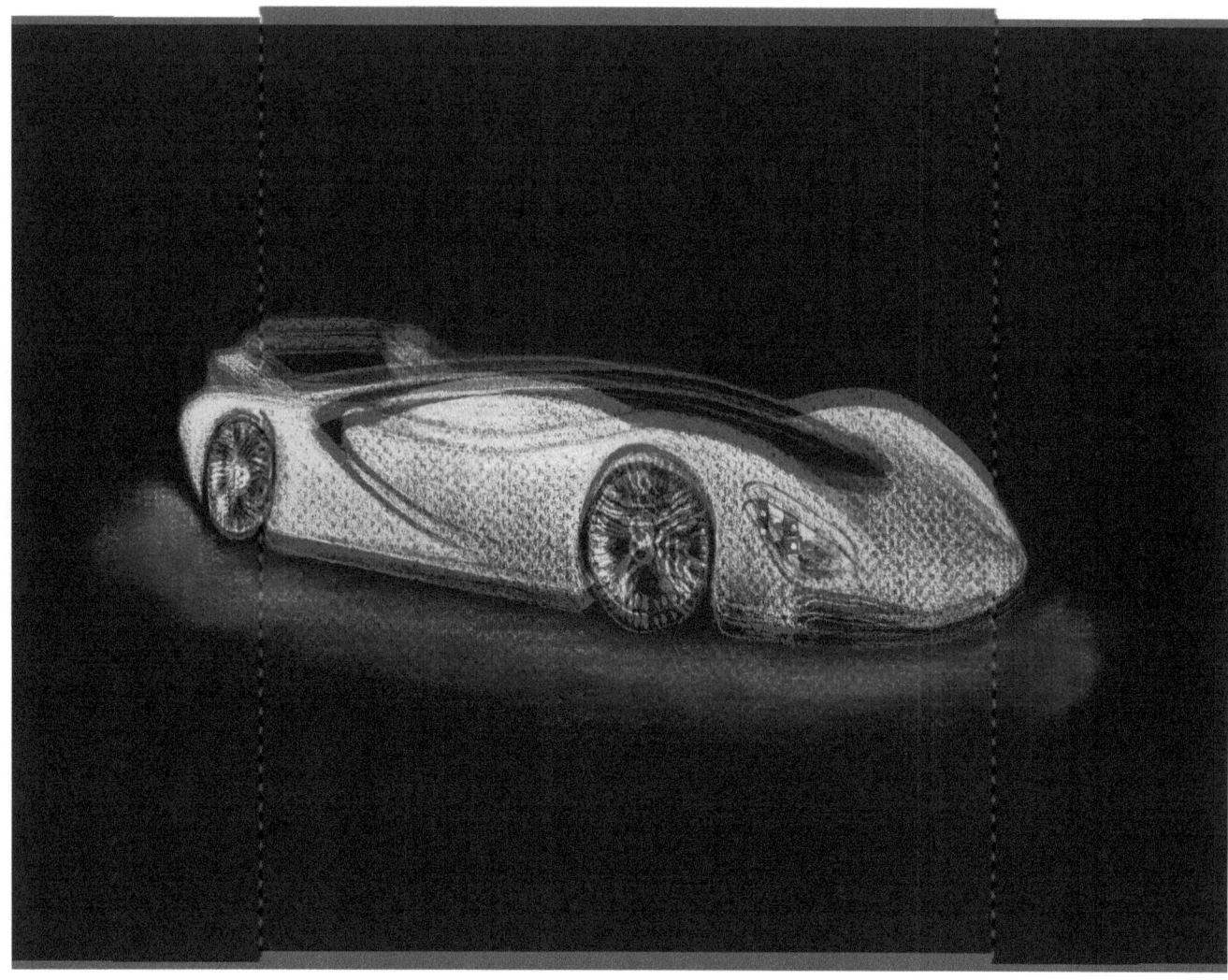

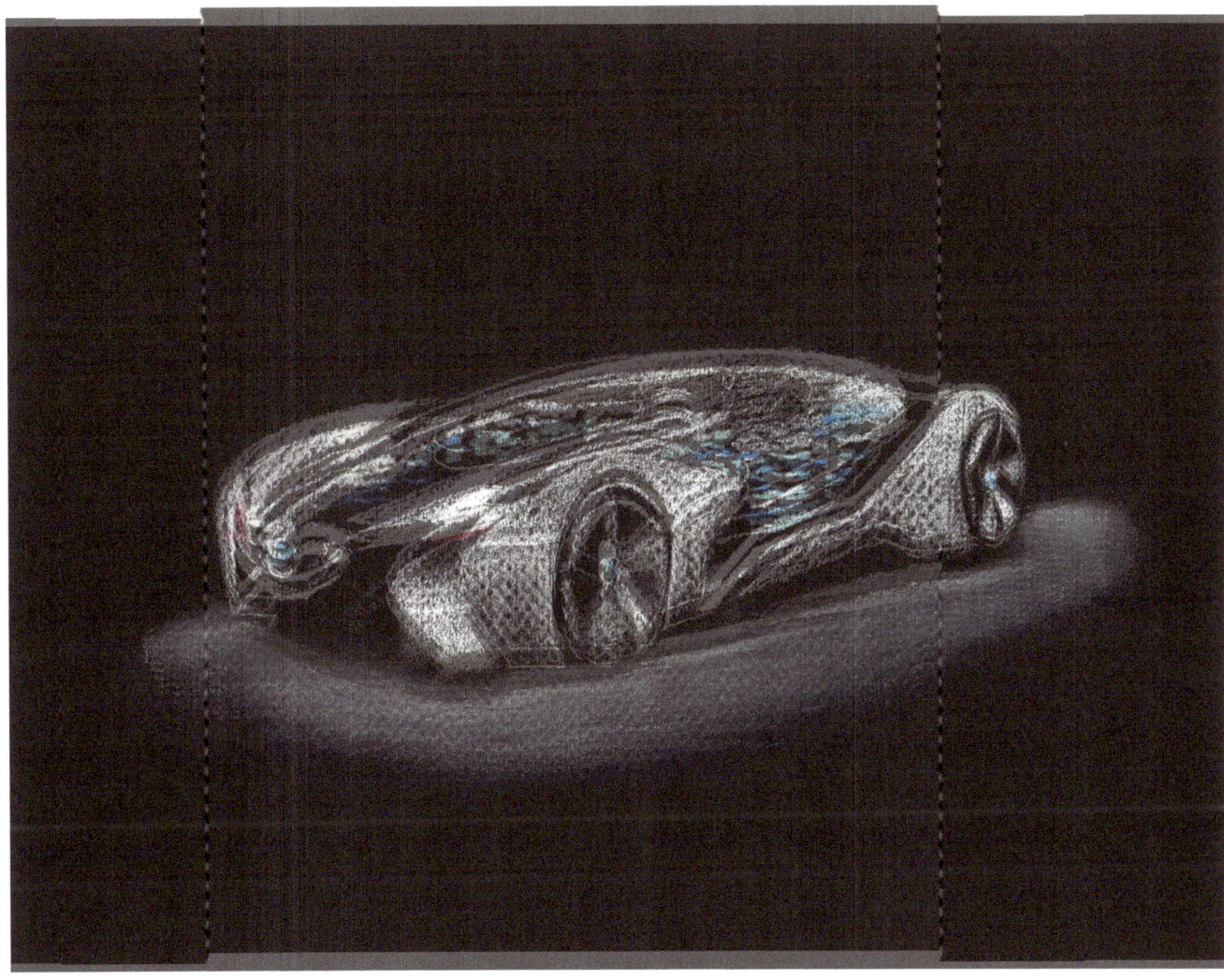

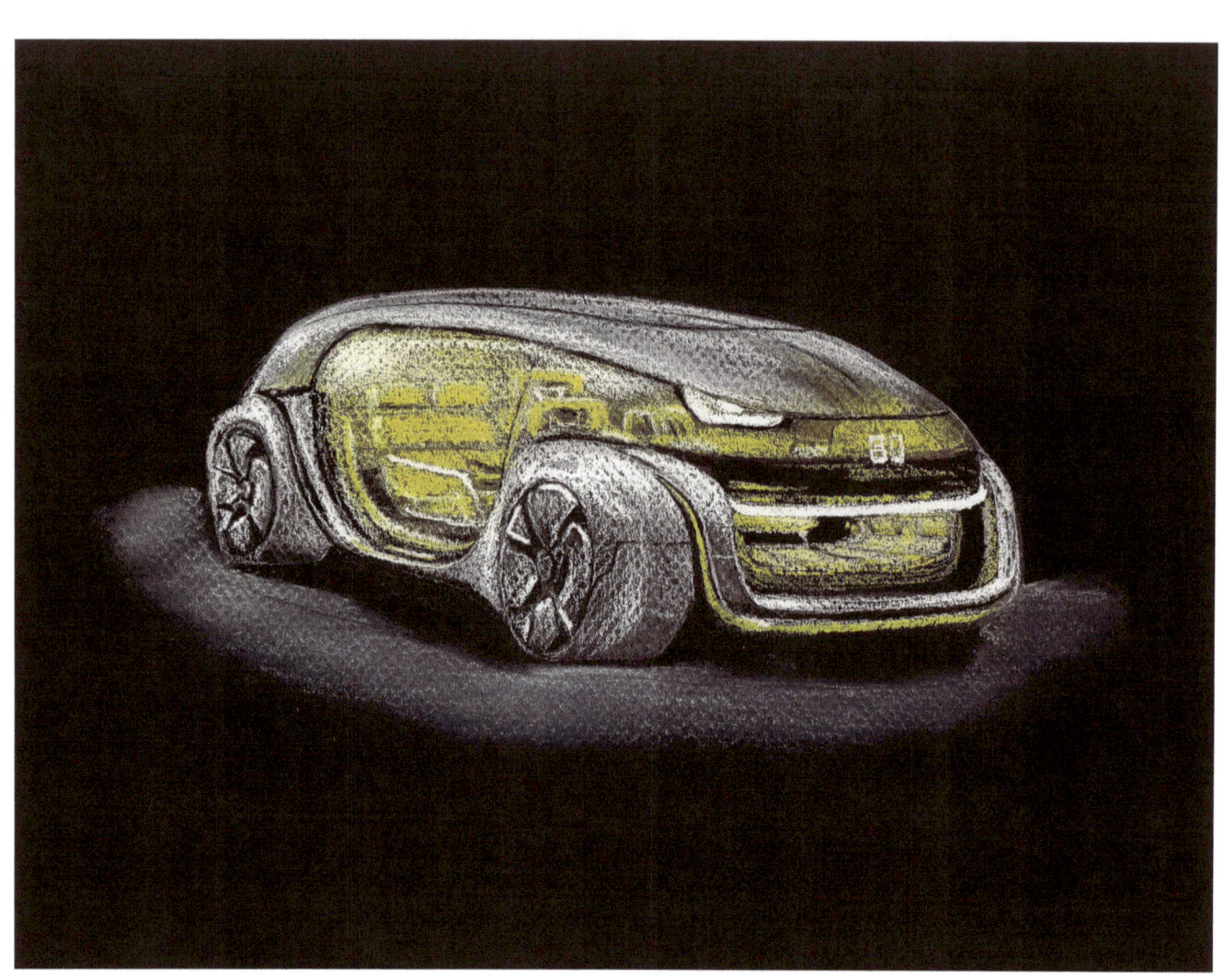

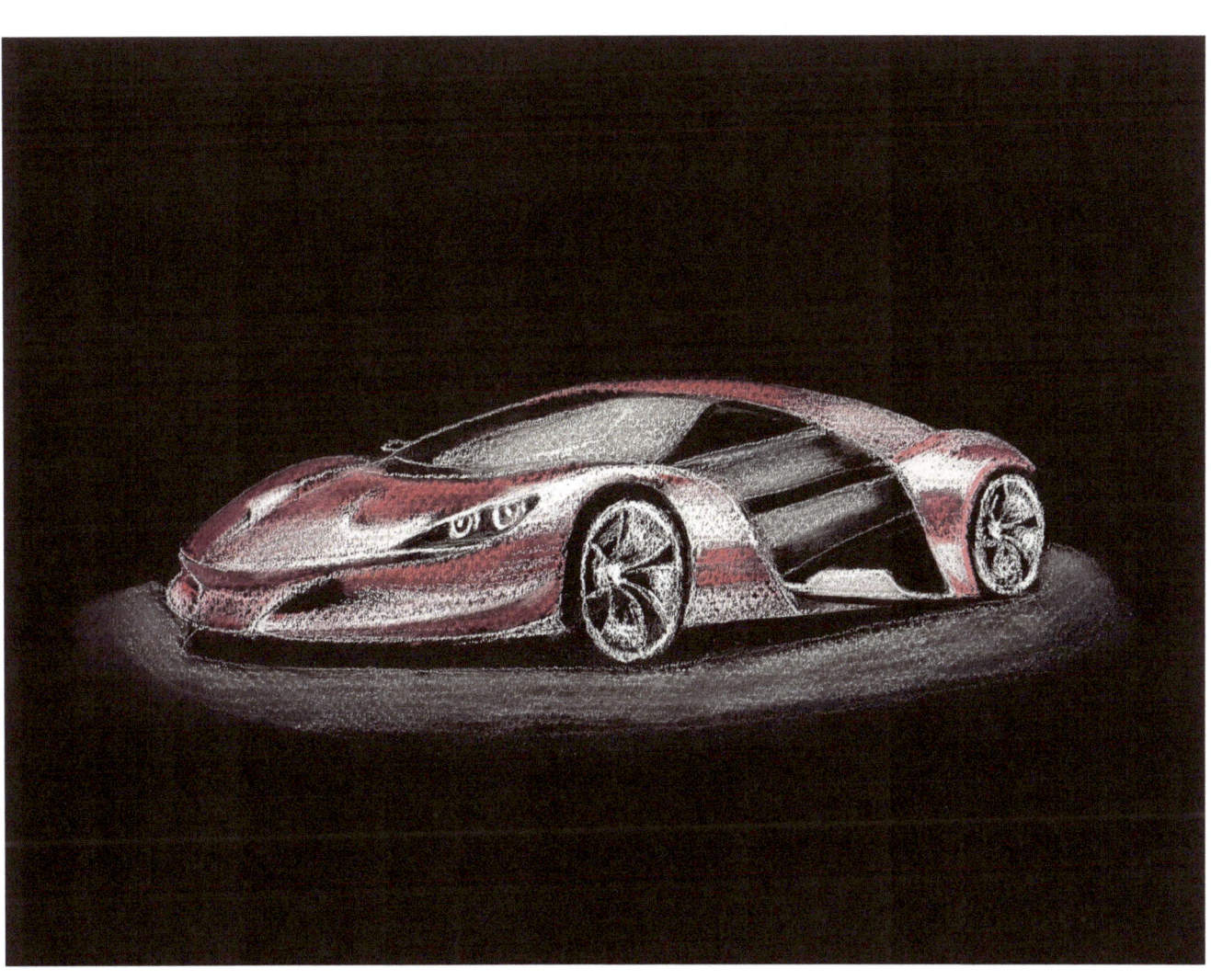

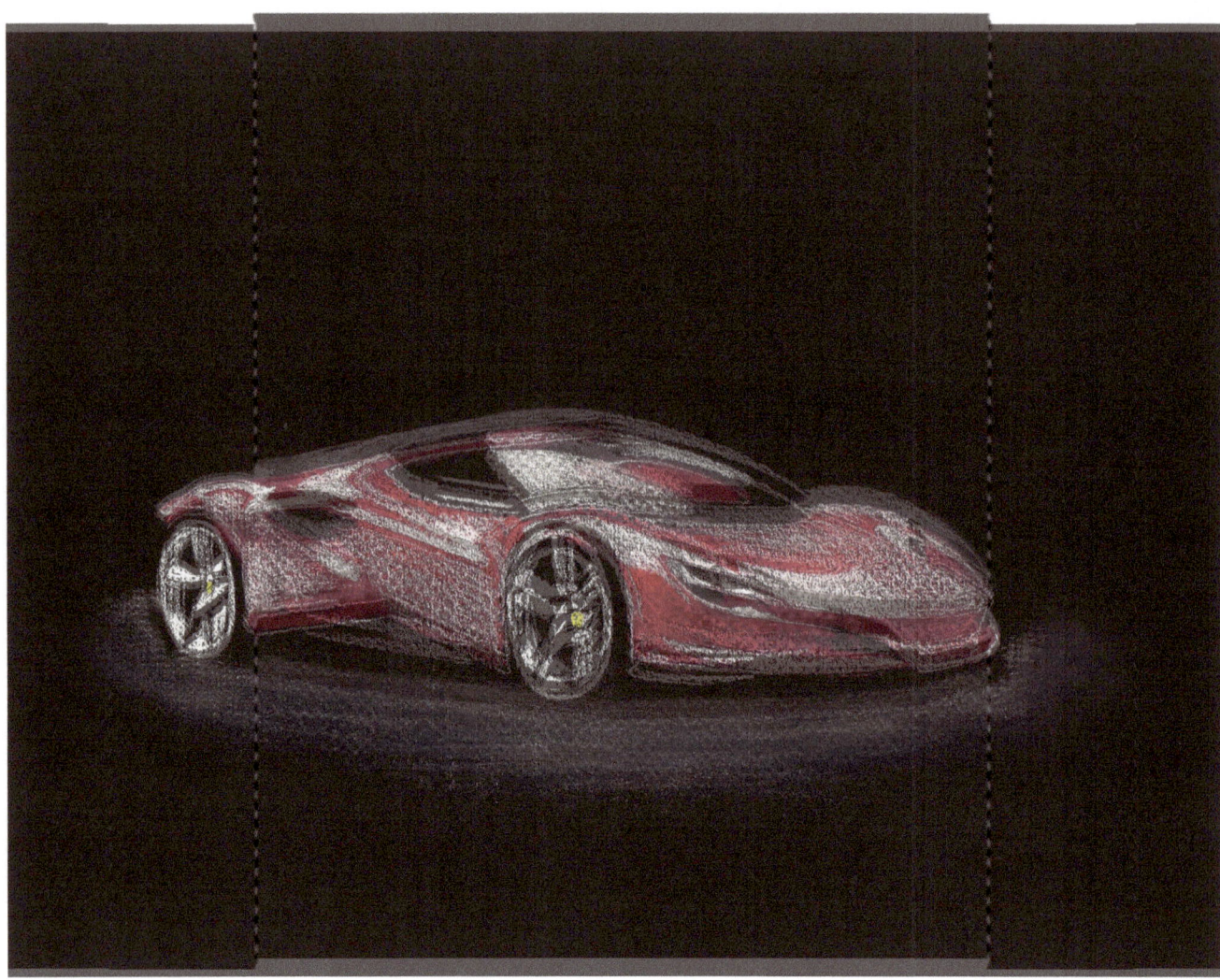

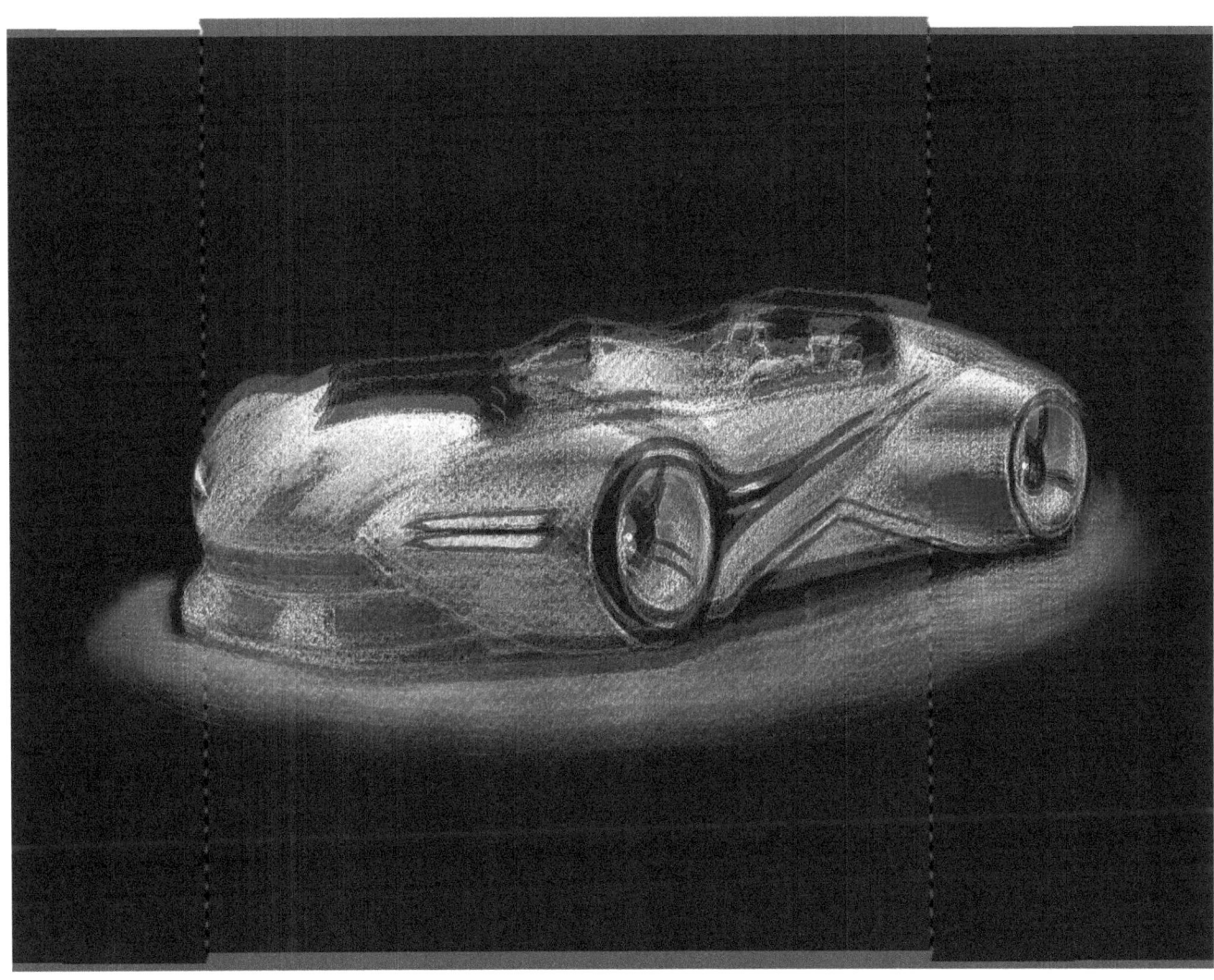

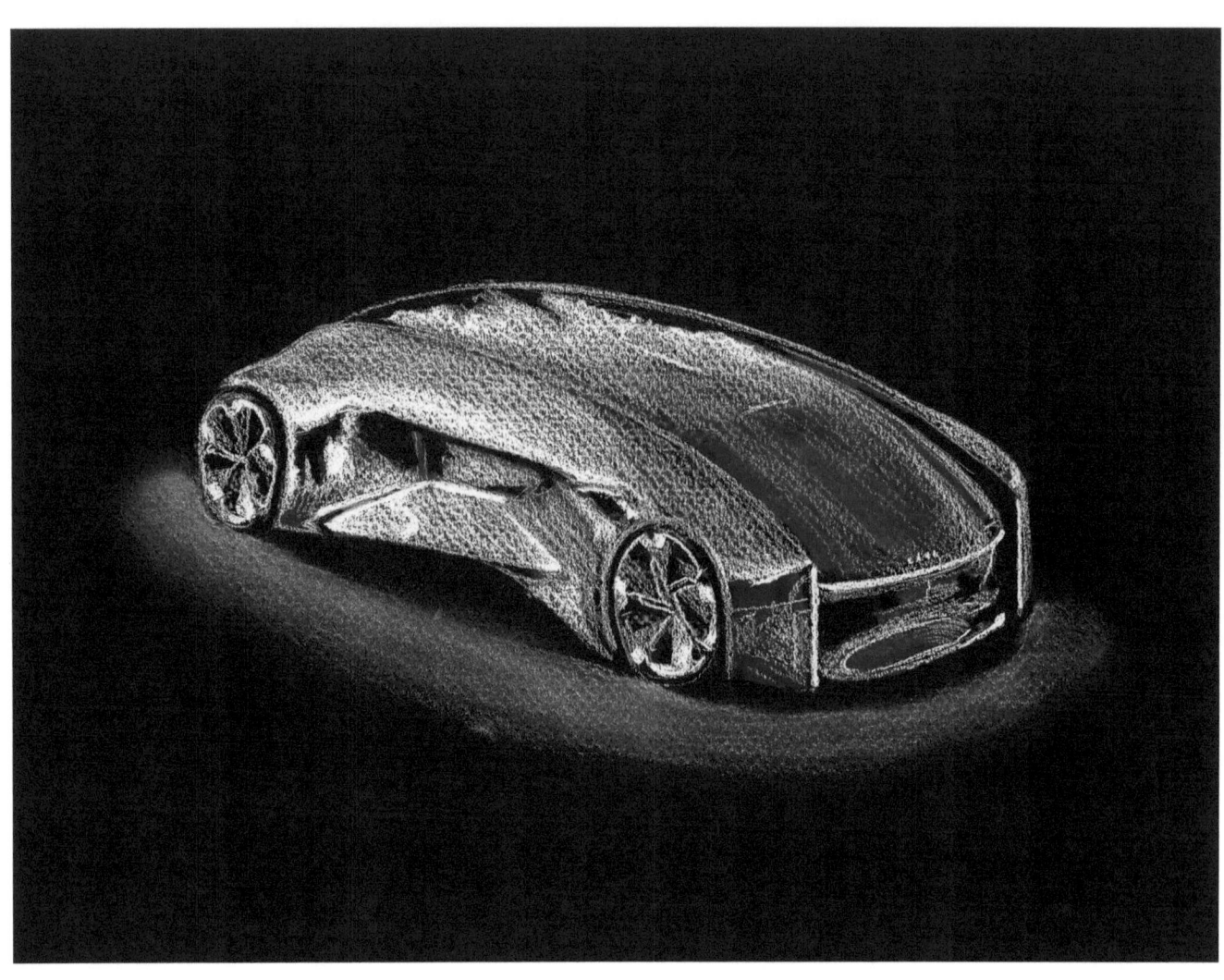

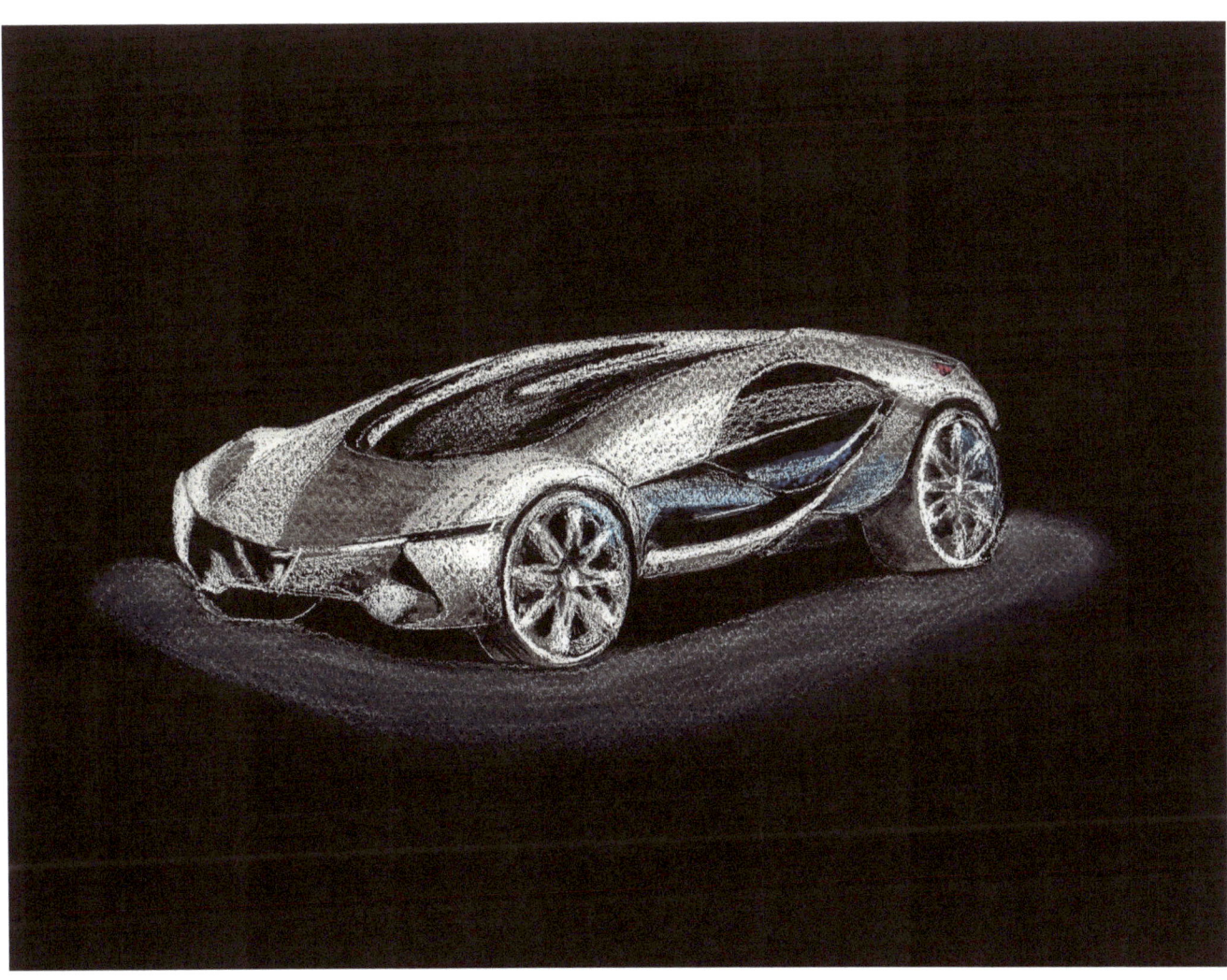

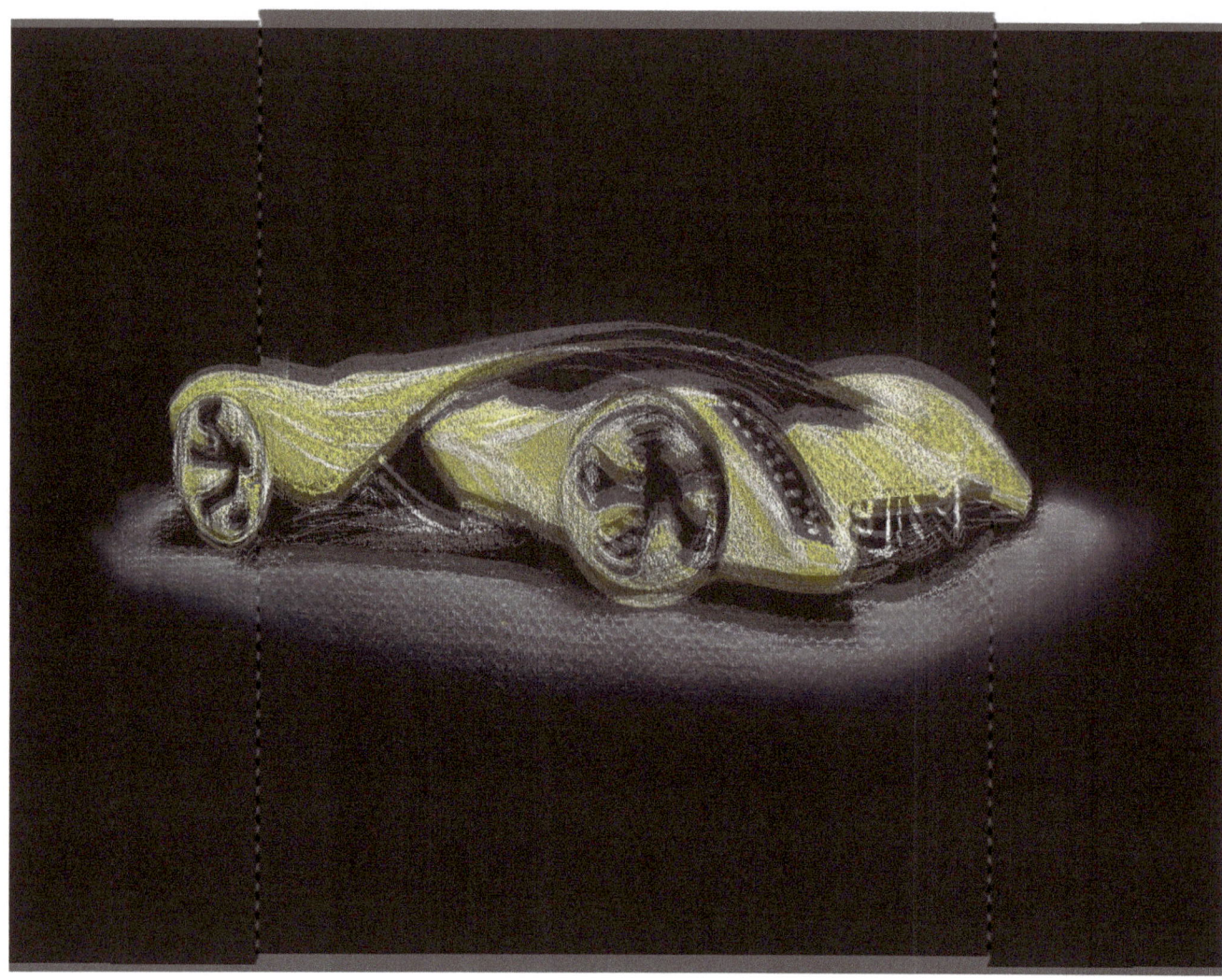

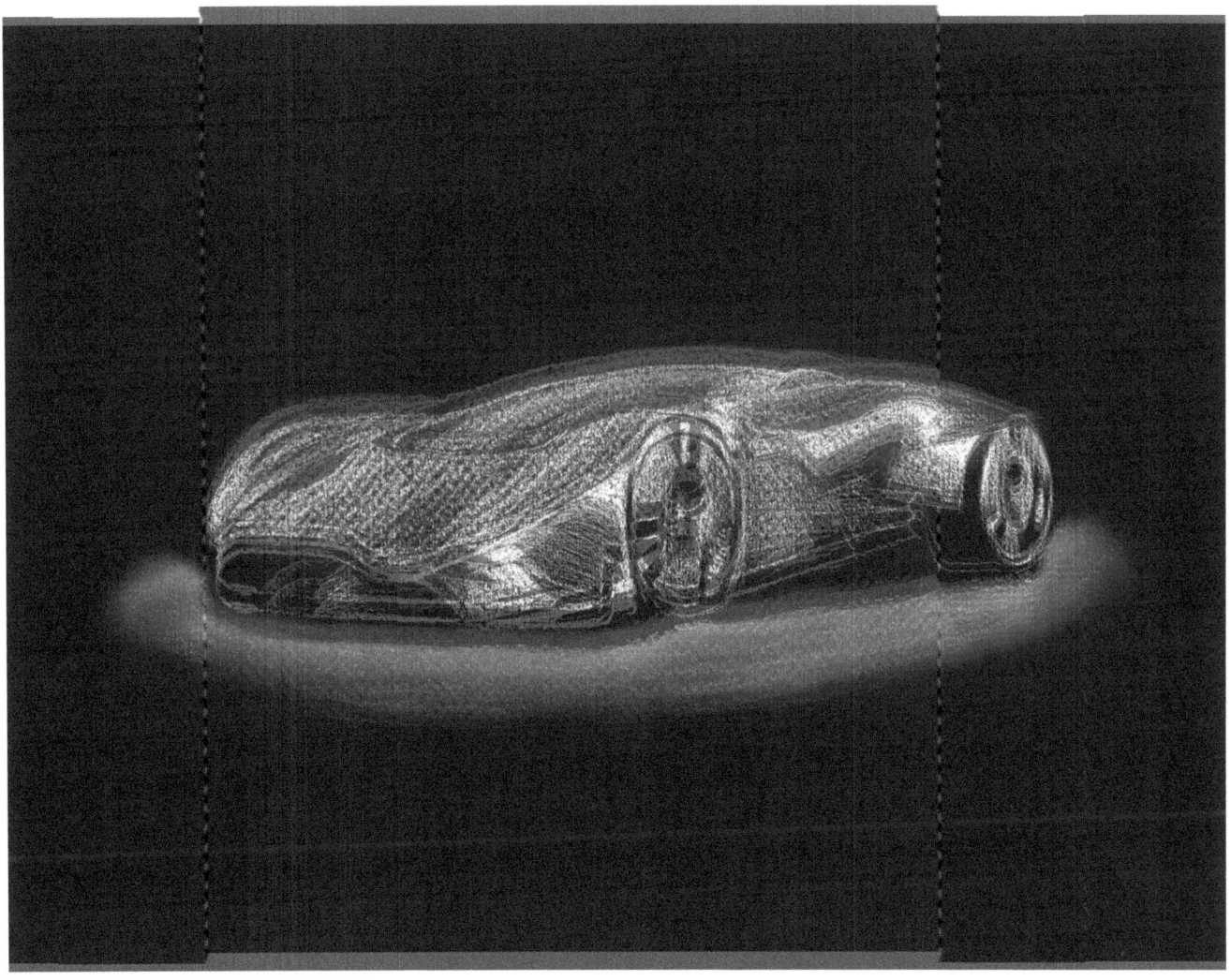

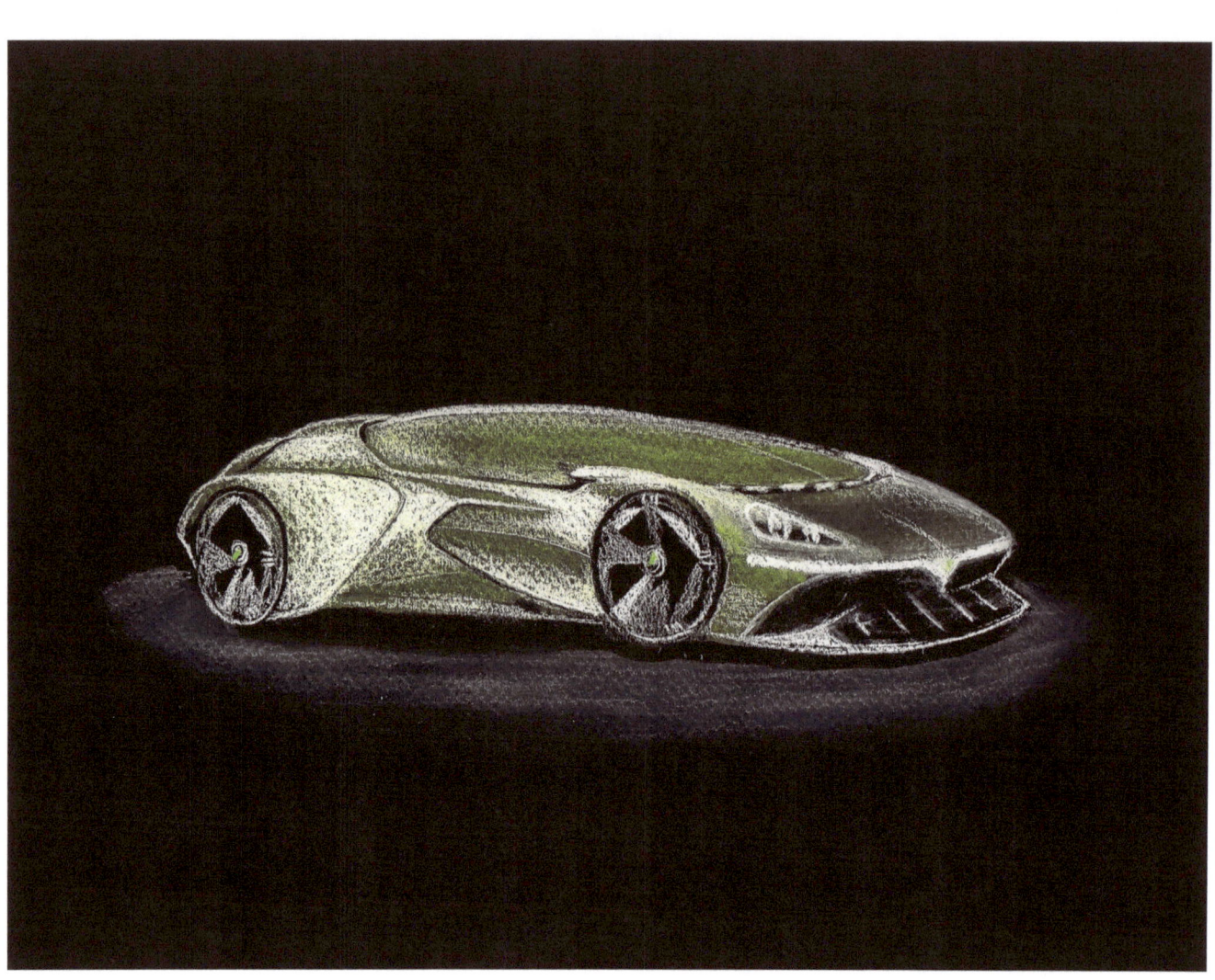

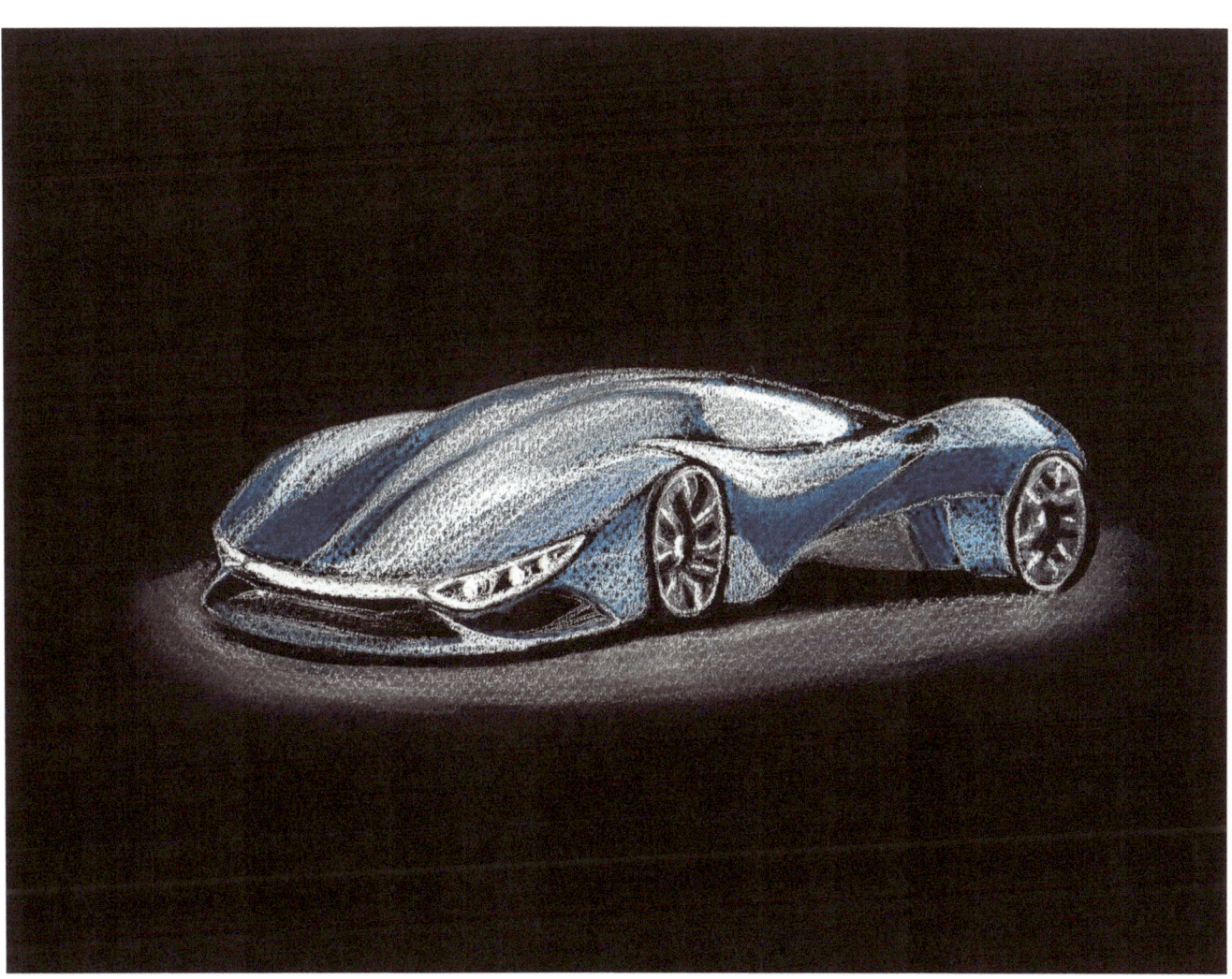

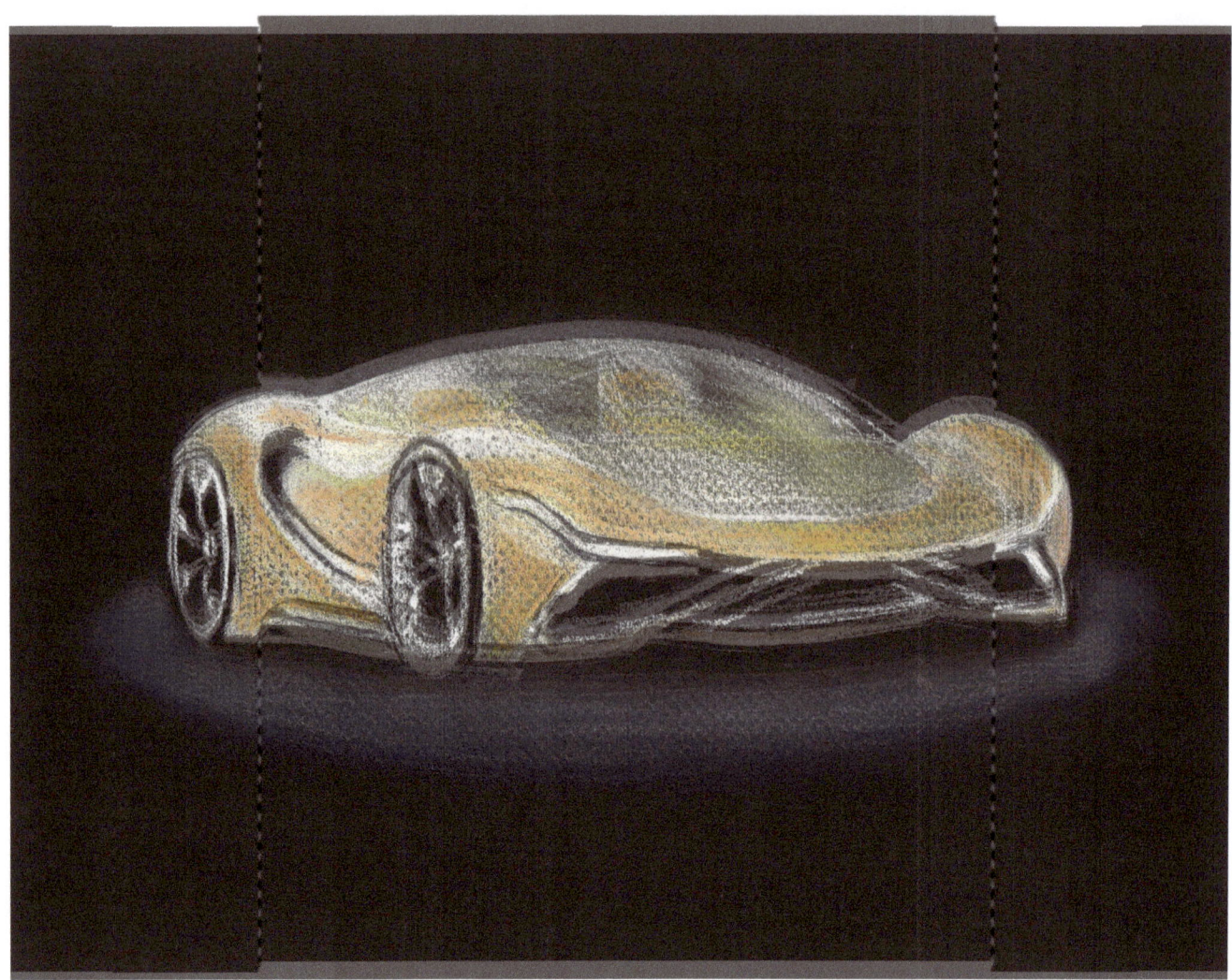

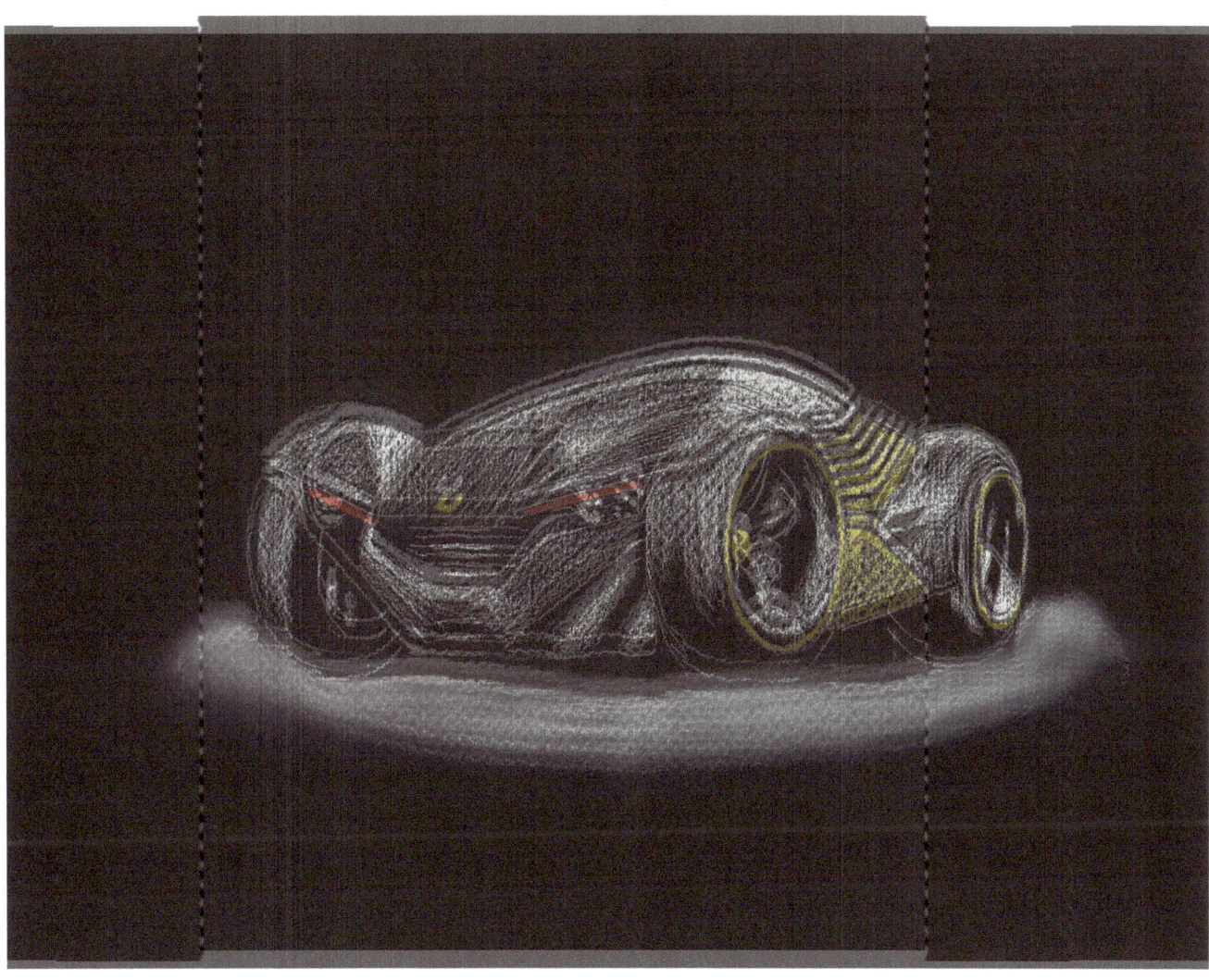

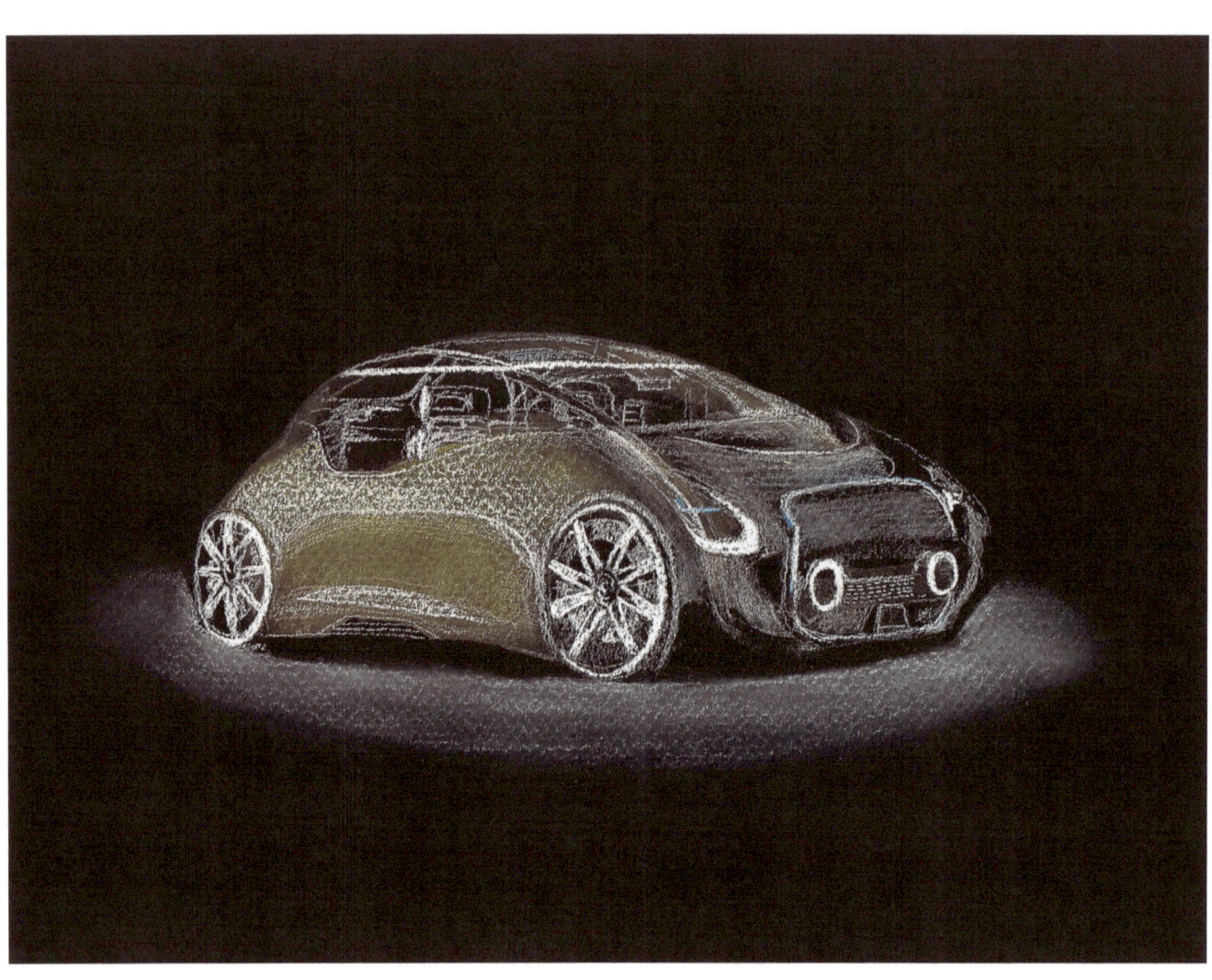

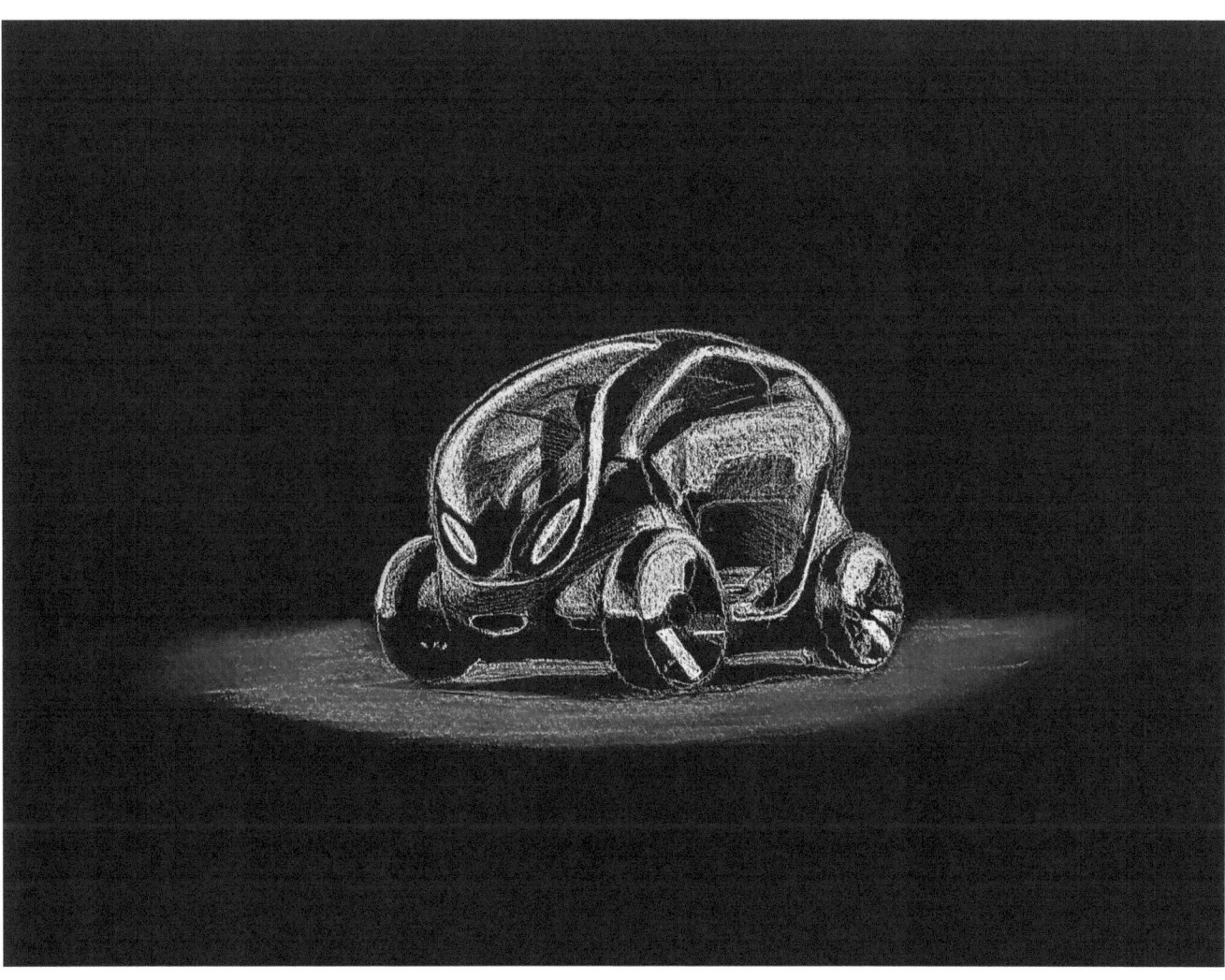

Check out more books from **Peter Wong** at www.amazon.com

LEGEND OF THE 12 ANIMALS

LEGEND OF THE 14 UNDERWATER CREATURES

DRAWING OF THE 14 AMAZING BIRDS

DRAWING OF THE 14 WILD ANIMALS

LET's DRAW CARTOONS-The 28 Cute Chibi Characters

DRAWING OF THE 14 FURRY FRIENDS

DESIGN OF THE 14 MODERN SHOES

PASTEL PAINTING OF THE 30 AMAZING CARS

More artworks from **Peter design** at www.Society6.com/PeterDesign

and online course of drawing at **www.Udemy.com**

https://www.udemy.com/course/mocalife_intro_pencil_drawing/?couponCode=SKILLS4SALEA

Check out more handmade crafts
from **MoCaLife design** at *www.MoCaLife.Etsy.com*

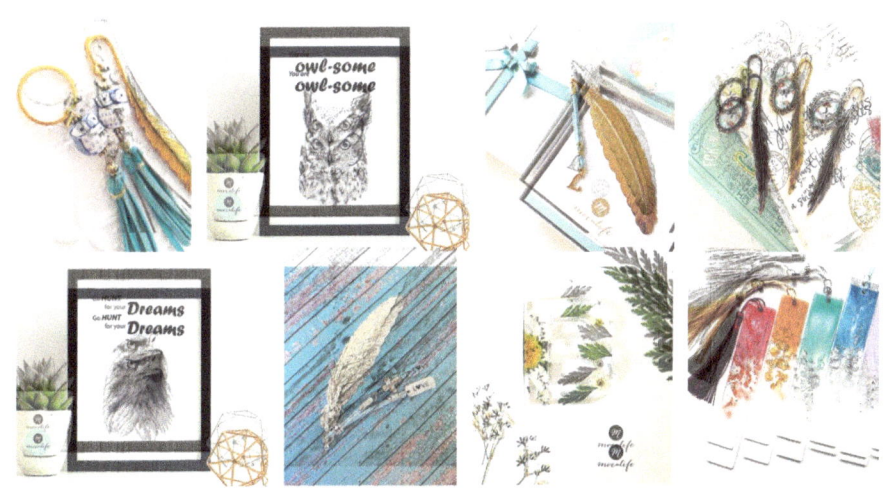

www.ingramcontent.com/pod-product-compliance
Lightning Source LLC
Chambersburg PA
CBHW051950210526

45474CB00003B/80